Off the Hook Too! casts a wide net...

Hunting—There is no arguing that antlers are important. They help deer decide who gets a date. They help successful hunters get a grip while dragging their prize from the woods. They are the ultimate Northwoods accent piece, suitable for hanging in any room but mostly those frequented by Northwoods men.

Photography—There is something horribly wrong with a society that requires its young to become certified in Hunter Safety before handling a gun, yet will put a fully loaded camera into a child's hands at a wedding and say, "Get a shot of Daddy doing the Chicken Dance!"

Berry picking—If someone asks if we've been picking blueberries, we say yes, because it's hard to lie when you have leaves in your hair and blue spots on your butt. When they ask where, we say "The Plains." Then we say "Goodbye." We're there to pick. It's the way of the sticks.

Toys—My particular generation is the baby boomers. We were born as a direct result of WWII. Our daddies were very happy to come home to our mommies. They expressed their joy by populating the earth with many children who were easily entertained.

Cell phones--"Don't those damn things ever stop ringin'?" my husband bellowed. Our son, seated beside him in the car, bent his head in obvious shame, focusing on the offending cell phone in his hand. A moment later his sister's cell phone rang in the back seat. It was her brother, calling her from the front.

Bugs—I opened the cap on my shampoo, and knew just how Janet Leigh felt when Norman Bates joined her for a shower in Psycho. There was an earwig underneath it, and it wasn't finished bathing. We are used to being bugged and having nowhere to hide. If Norman had made his move on a Maki in the sauna, she'd have parted his hair with a pickaxe.

Food—There is a time and a place for eating healthier. I have no idea when or where that is, but I am pretty sure it's not Thanksgiving Day, when every dish is meant to shine, mainly from its high fat content. We are thankful for giblet gravy and real butter.

Barbie—In the beginning, she was blonde or brunette. Then she became black or Hispanic, which was a good thing. Then you cut her hair, which was a bad thing because it devalued your investment and caused Ken to lose interest, though nobody thought Ken was much of a catch, anyway.

Data breach—What makes a data breach even more frightening is that 400 of our personal, private characteristics may also be fully exposed. The computing element may, at this very moment, be tuning into the facts that you are a smoker and a dog owner. What are they going to do? Sniff you out and steal your dog?

Crafting—It was a controlled burn, but just barely. The wood burner warmed up faster than the artist, from "cool" to "incinerate" before I could warm my coffee. When the smoke finally cleared, I keenly perceived with my artist's eye that I had succeeded in creating charcoal. And it wasn't even good-looking charcoal.

Bathrooms—Ever since the outhouse found its way in, man has struggled to delicately define his waste space. The new spa-like bathroom isn't a place where you just go. Well, it kind of is, but you also go there to relax, unwind and pamper yourself while family members try to beat the door down because they need to take care of business.

Grandparenting—My mom never played canasta, but she didn't roll around on the floor with our kids, either, because old grandmothers had something NEW grandmothers lack: their dignity. My mom raised her eyebrows, said stuff like "Oh dear," and kicked naked Barbies under the couch to be with their clothes. Naked Kens, too, different couch.

Guilt—Not to brag (sin of pride), but we Catholics have kind of cornered the market on guilt. Catholics can confess our sins to a priest and receive penance--prayer, more or less of it, depends on the week-- to wipe our slates clean. Then we walk out of the confessional, speculate on why the next guy is going in, and bam! We're back in the red again.

Off the Hook Too!

Off-Beat Reporter's Tales from Michigan's U.P.

Nancy Besonen

Modern History Press

Ann Arbor, MI

Off the Hook Too!: Off-Beat Reporter's Tales from Michigan's U.P.

Copyright © 2024 by Nancy Besonen. All Rights Reserved

ISBN 978-1-61599-825-8 paperback
ISBN 978-1-61599-826-5 hardcover
ISBN 978-1-61599-827-2 eBook

Modern History Press   info@ModernHistoryPress.com
5145 Pontiac Trail   www.ModernHistoryPress.com
Ann Arbor, MI 48105   Tollfree 888-761-6268

Distributed by INGRAM Book Group (USA/CAN/EU/AU)

MODERN
HISTORY
PRESS

Thank you, God, for everything

Edith Rutter-Leatham

*also, Mrs. Haberichter's kindergarten class
before our milk & cookies*

Contents

1. WE THE PEOPLE..1
   DATELINE: D.C. & DeKalb 1
   Wonder Woman vs. HB 3
   A Hit for Everyman 4
   Above Average Inauguration..7

2. PET PEEVES 9
   It's a Jungle in Here 9
   Dogs Show Me Up 11
   "Blackie" Rises Again 13

3. MIXED BAG 15
   Asteroid Alert 15
   Hacker Shares Helpful Hints...17
   Pinata Down!..18
   Pronunciation Primer 19
   Calling Mr. President...21
   Prone From Accidents 23

4. WILD THINGS...27
   Crop Adjuster Breaches Security 27
   Hooked on Hunting..29
   'Twas the Second Week of Deer Camp 31
   Deer With a Difference 33
   Talking Turkey 34

5. REEL ME IN..37
   Digging Up Bones 37
   Write a Winning Fish Tale 38
   Is Trout Worship Wrong?..40
   Fish Camp Goes Co-ed 42
   Fresh Spin on Fish Camping...44

6. AT OUR SERVICE 47
   Dad has Shuttle Seniority 47
   In a Military State..48
   Living the Dream 51
   Bringing Home World War II 53

7. PURSUIT OF FRUIT 55

Pails in Comparison..55
Berry Picker Blues 57
How We Like Them Apples 59

8. THINGS OF BEAUTY 61
Capris Here—Run for Cover! 61
Oscars Out of Fashion 63
Mr. Rogers Rocked It 64
"Alien Stompers" All the Rage...66

9. MUSIC TO MY EARS...69
Campbell Strikes a Chord 69
We Want Another Rock?...72
Disco Drops the Ball 73

10. FUN WITH FADS 75
Barbie Gets Her Grooves On 75
Swedes Make a Clean Sweep 77
Real Fake News..78
Guerilla Artist Crosses Lines 80
Spa Bathrooms Waste Space 82
Weather Poodle Alert..83
From Mouths of Babes...85

11. DEALING WITH WHEELING 87
Road Gators Bite 87
Caroling Car on a Roll 88
"Dusty Rose" Hits the Trail..90
Where's the Grease?..93
Dirty Driving 94
Ready, Set, Mow! 96

12. FEAR IS WHY WE'RE HERE......................................99
My Computer is Dying! 99
Revenge of the Refrigerator 100
Cobras Can't Touch Us...102
Reporters are Replaceable..104
Data Thief Disappointment..105
Fear is our Friend..107

13. PUTTING THE MISS IN CHRISTMAS...........................109
Just Use Money! 109
Testing, Testing 111
Christmas is for Crafters..113
Checkers, Anyone? 114

Three Kings Rule 116
It's Another Perfect Tree 117

14. WHAT'S BUGGING US 121
    Nowhere to Hide 121
    Bees Do It 123
    The Third Plague 124
    We're the Most Invasive 125

15. FOOD FOR AUGHT 129
    Weighing In on Lists 129
    Beer's Getting Winey 130
    Flying High on Chocolate 131
    Mutiny From our Bounty 133
    Shame on Turkeys 135

16. FAMILY MATTERS 137
    Speaking of Dad 137
    Working, With Children 138
    Focus on Photography 141
    Family Banking Doesn't Pay 143
    Tot Translator 145
    NEW Grandmothers Rock & Roll 146
    No Escaping Sunday School 148

17. OLDER, NO WISER 151
    Getting Gamey 151
    Gripers Go Pro 152
    Lifetime Loser 154
    Do You Wah Diddy? 156
    The Future is Calling 157

18. LAST WORDS 159
    War of the Words 159
    Lassie, Come Back! 160
    Live Guilt-Free 162
    Canada Makes Change 163
    Fun With Forecasting 165
    Fisherman's Guide to Foul Weather 166
    I'm Not THAT Shopper 166

About the Author 169

Watton, Michigan and Local Area

1. Watton
2. Covington
3. Vermilac Lake
4. L'Anse
5. Baraga
6. Keweenaw Bay

Michigan's Upper Peninsula

1. WE THE PEOPLE

DATELINE: D.C. & DeKalb

DATELINE: D.C.--I heard such a funny news story last week, I had to commit it to memory. Unfortunately, it was my memory, a sieve that couldn't hold the Eastern Seaboard, but I vaguely recall the gist.

It was about our Nation's Capital, and how it was shut down for four days due to the blizzard raging in Washington, D.C. Lawmakers got those days off, which cost the country millions of dollars in lost business--just slightly less than it would have cost if they could have gotten into their offices and conducted business as usual.

But that was not the funny part. The funny part was when the newsman said, "Essential staff are still required to come in." He was not talking about the president, senators, representatives, elephants, donkeys, etc. that make up our fair democracy. He was talking about the janitors.

As a proud American who used to clean the multi-purpose building in Covington, which houses a gym, kitchen, dining area, office and bathrooms, I would like to take this opportunity to announce: No Street Shoes in the Gym!

Thank you. That has been building up inside of me for a long time, ever since our three kids were little enough to come with me and play "Hop the Mop." They'd stand in a row on the gym's center line while I came tearing across the floor at them, pushing a three-foot-wide dust mop aimed right at their feet.

At the very last minute, they'd hop the mop. Sometimes, playing upon their innocence and my superior cunning, I'd do a little hesitation step and knock them all down like bowling pins. I so miss having little ones about. Can't wait for grandkids!

As I was typing, even though outside conditions were not suitable for man nor beast nor lawmakers, essential staff still had to report for duty last week. While the Wheels of Justice spun in the snow, they kept the Capital running like clockwork: shoveling, firing the stoves, and mopping up imaginary strikes starring our Supreme Court justices.

Or did they?

For four stormy days, essential staff ruled. I am not typing that they actually ran our country during that period. I am typing that I would have liked to see them try. As they say in the business, "One hand washes the other, and both hands scrub the Floor."

Essential staff would put up a unified front, because they know if you don't take care of business by the end of the day, people will be tripping over their trash. If essential staffers indulged in partisanship, they might have constituents, but they wouldn't have any customers.

The implications would be staggering: the keys to the free world in the hands of the common man! World peace was surely within our grasp, along with sensible spending and having to kick your shoes off before coming into the House.

Then the storm in Washington passed, and non-essential staff were all called back to work.

DATELINE: DeKALB--The Washington snow scoop was still making newsmen swoon when another big story broke, this one much closer to home. An earthquake caused our very own Midwest to shudder. My brother, Mark, was there. This headline was mine!

It happened last Wednesday, and the quake's epicenter was in Kane County, IL. Depending upon your news source, it registered anywhere from a 3.8 to a 4.3. It rattled the corn cobs right in their husks--a few kernels may have even popped--and was felt as far away as Chicago.

Mark, a retired Army major who lives perilously close to the source in DeKalb, IL, said it was no great shakes.

"Yeah, we used to have earthquakes bigger than that every day in Alaska," Mark said in a live telephone interview, displaying no regard whatsoever for my career aspirations. "It didn't even wake me up."

"Work with me, man," I begged. "Any casualties in the neighborhood? Cracks in the foundation? Pictures hanging crooked in the hallway? DID THE DOG MESS THE RUG?"

"Nope. You talk to Ma lately? How's she doin'?"

What does Mark know about tremors? He drinks more coffee than I do. We register better than a 3.8 before our first cup of the day. An earthquake would just make us think we're sitting still for a change.

The national news reporters didn't seem to fare much better. Maybe they talked to Mark, too, because the *Snow Scoop in Washington* totally upstaged the *Tragedy in the Heartland*. That's what I'm calling it, just for practice, because someday my boat is bound to come in.

When it does, I've got just the mop for cleaning up in its aftermath. Watch your feet.

Wonder Woman vs. HB

If you feel empowered by Wonder Woman, cross your wrists in front of you and prepare to deflect bullets, because I am about to take some cheap shots.

I can't help myself. I feel empowered, too.

Wonder Woman is the newest marvel to leap straight out of comic books and onto the big screen. She is the daughter of Zeus, king of the gods, and Queen Hippolyta, an Amazon warrior who has superpowers and a wardrobe that is a tad scanty.

Wonder Woman also sports some serious accessories, including bullet-proof cuffs and a magic lasso. And last weekend she used all of the above, but mostly her wardrobe, to "break the glass ceiling" for women directors by breaking box office records.

I know all about glass ceilings. I learned about them from the Sokero brothers of Finland, who were visiting family in the U.P. They also visited Shute's Bar in Calumet, which boasts an historic stained-glass canopy which I intend to toast, for history's sake of course, the very next time we are in town.

But I would never dream of breaking the ceiling at Shute's, because I am not a much-oppressed female director. I am not even an oppressed female reporter. I get to cover both sports and news. And I can even write about Wonder Woman after I get my real work done.

That is because Wonder Woman is making big news these days by empowering women. We finally have an action figure we can look up to, though I personally find Robert Downey Jr. even more fetching as Iron Man. Hear us roar!

According to popular media, wherever there are movie screens, women are taking their daughters to see Wonder Woman. Women are renting theaters for "girls only" screenings. And women are already planning a Wonder Woman sequel, hopefully co-starring Robert Downey Jr. as Iron Man.

I am a bit reluctant to take my daughters to a movie about a woman who doesn't duck bullets and is banned from Schute's Bar for what she's doing to glass ceilings. That is why they will be joining me this week for a limited run at Fish Camp in Mercer, WI.

Nobody is oppressed at Fish Camp, not even the fish. Everyone dresses sensibly, in clothes we seldom bother changing unless we are headed to town. Then we dress better above the watering line, which would be the bar at the Northwoods Bar.

We are all Wonder Women (and men) at Fish Camp! We wonder where the fish are. We wonder how to turn off the fire alarm when we are cooking in the cabin. We wonder why the White Sox are losing and the Cubs aren't, because we all hail from Chicago's South Side.

And my daughters will wonder, too, at my spinners that deflect fish, my magical fishing rod that separates in the middle when I make a long cast, and my aluminum beer koozie of doom engraved with the mysterious letters, "HB." Because some wonders, like my hard-earned Fish Camp nickname, are best kept that way.

A Hit for Everyman

They were coming into town from out of state, out of country and in some cases, totally out of character to help America pick up the pieces of its lost national pastime.

And do you know what the headlines announced when they arrived?

"Welcome, imposters!"

I slapped my car horn in disgust when I heard the report on Minnesota Public Radio, causing an oncoming driver to smile, wave, and watch for hidden police cars over the next few miles. Talk about your misguided, bullheaded ingrates. Foul ball, I say!

Pro baseball players had gone on strike, protesting a proposed salary cap, and some club managers were striking back, calling up second, third and never-even-been-on-the-stringers to try to salvage the major league baseball season.

Players were also being harvested from amateur leagues, foreign teams and some sagging floral couches to which they thought they had successfully retired: "Yer' re-hired! Play ball!"

The season-saving strategy had thrown many fans into a real snit. They enjoy a steady diet of watching the pros play ball. Although it's proving an increasingly too rich diet for the fans, who have to eat but mostly drink in the parking lot before the game, they're not willing to change it.

Speaking from that neutral zone called the U.P., where the nearest major league ballpark is located downstate, which is technically out-of-

The crowd is riveted by the action as Dad scores a hit for everyman (on his team) in kickball

state, I don't really care. I lost my interest in baseball after I grew too old to play it in Chicago's Marquette Park.

However, if some adult who hasn't outgrown it suddenly picks up a bat and decides he wants to hit a ball with it, I for one am not going to stand in his way. And if we have to have heroes, then maybe it's high time we had some we can relate to.

Imagine somebody you could beat in a foot race ambling up to the plate, assuming an unthreatening batting stance, and then accidentally popping the ball over the outfielders' heads. It's a hit for everyman! The crowd goes wild!

After landing safe on first and catching his breath, the player accepts his thanks with a humble nod and a hint of a grin. He does not spit. He wouldn't know where to scratch. I think he's Gary Cooper in that old Lou Gehrig movie.

On the darker side, consider the real reason most of us tune into professional sports. Are we interested in seeing a football soar between two goal posts? Do we stare at the finish line to see which car will cross it first? Are we gentle-natured, caring, and basically humane? I think not!

It's not the "Hooray's!" but the "Oh, noooo's!" that nourish our baser selves, and just think of the feast a roster full of amateurs could serve up. Yes, it is good to see a play of the week, but it is far better to see a blooper, even though the player is making more while screwing up than we are by doing our jobs right.

Tune into the evening news, and you'll find that immediately following the game highlights, there is sometimes an even longer replay of spectacular blunders. Outstanding interceptions and slam dunks are things of beauty, but for pure entertainment, you can't beat a scapegoat. Trust me, I know.

Two years ago, I was treading on thin ice on Keweenaw Bay, looking for an angler to interview, when I met a former Green Bay Packer. I got the big story--the fish were biting!--then later, called the Football Hall of Fame in Green Bay, WI for a few sentences about his playing career.

I found I'd hooked a whopper.

The man at the museum recounted Chester Marcol's long and glowing career, including a history-making play by the former place kicker. In the 1980 season opener, in overtime vs. the Chicago Bears, Marcol scored the winning touchdown when he caught his own blocked field goal kick and ran it into the end zone.

It was an "Oh, noooo!" and a "Hooray!", all in the same play. As for Marcol, he cared more about the fishing. He was a pro a person could look up to--that is, when he wasn't hunkered down, fishing through his hole in the ice.

And we could look up to our amateurs, too, those unlikely boys of summer ready and willing to come up to the plate. Given a shot, they'd thrill us with their occasional triumphs and reassure us with the rest, because a swing and a miss in the bigs is still a hit for everyman.

Above Average Inauguration

NASHVILLE, TN, Jan. 2020—Sarah Fuller, the first woman to score in a Power Five conference football game, says she's been invited to attend President-elect Joe Biden's inauguration on Wednesday.
From the preceding AP news brief, we may conclude that:

1. Sarah Fuller sure can kick.

2. Sarah Fuller has broken an important barrier, allowing girls everywhere to someday realize their dream of attending a presidential inauguration.

3. Invitation-wise, it's not looking good for the rest of us.

While it's probably not the worst capital offense committed in Washington this past week, we still feel the sting from being left out. The reason for the unfortunate oversight is, the rest of us are just your average Americans.

We touch all the bases—work, pay bills, carpool, remove stains—without ever hearing the roar of the crowd. The only recognition we receive is a head-butt from the cat, and we have to pop a can of the good stuff to score it.

Later that night, he will gak it up on the living room rug because our cat is average, too, and can't stomach a rich diet. Which is quite possibly why cats didn't make the cut either for invitations to President-elect Joe Biden's inauguration.

The irony of the situation is, cats don't particularly care. Also, average Americans are the people who made the inauguration possible, standing in long lines for an above-average amount of time to elect the President-elect.

So, if We the Average People can't attend the presidential inauguration, then who can?

As a highly trained watchdog for the public (I have a journalism degree!), I made it my personal priority to track down the list of who scored a ticket to the inauguration. My strategy consisted of typing progressively sterner commands into my computer until it finally spat it out, just like the cat.

Here's what I got: Due to the pandemic, this year's invitation list has been whittled down, from the usual 200,000 guests to just 1,500. Members of Congress can bring one friend each. Sarah can come. So can Joe and Kamala. Mike is a yes. Donald is a no.

Beyond that, I got nothin'.

The good news is, the event will be televised, and everyone is created equal in the eyes of TV advertisers, as long as we've paid our cable/dish/satellite/electric bill. We all have front row seats to the gala, which will feature above-average performers, politicians included.

Lady Gaga will sing the Star-Spangled Banner. Jennifer Lopez will perform some of her greatest hits. Bruce Springsteen, Jon Bon Jovi and Justin Timberlake are all on the program, too, hosted by actor Tom Hanks.

If you look really hard and can see past all the hoopla, you might even spot Sarah Fuller in the audience, kicking back and enjoying the show.

2. PET PEEVES

It's a Jungle in Here

It's 8 a.m., and Franklin wants out of the office place. Franklin expresses his dissatisfaction by leaping up onto my desk to dolefully gaze out the window at Bob, who wants back into the office place.

Franklin is one bad cat. Bob is the other one.

I cannot work under these conditions, which is obvious by the work that I do. Yet every day I am forced to share my office with a bunch of animals that are not my co-workers at the newspaper. This, my friends, is why our future is doomed.

I read all about it in *Time* magazine awhile back because my sister-in-law got a free subscription and figures I need more input. Though *Time* is seriously lacking in its junior high sports and senior cribbage scores coverage, it really shines at hard news, like *The Future of Working*.

According to my input, work as we know it will not exist in the future. We'll zip out to the office with jet packs strapped to our backs, push buttons all day and then return home exhausted to our boy, Elroy and slobbery dog, Astro.

Wait! That's *The Jetsons*, a futuristic cartoon from our past. Instead of jet packs, we'll have home offices. We'll barely have to budge to go to work. Our rear ends will be the size of Volkswagens, but work will be more flexible, freelance, and collaborative. Our 40-hour work week could even be whittled down to 30.

(So might our pay. That's why we'll have to freelance, collaborating with our teenage co-worker at McDonald's who wants extra shifts to pay for prom).

Women will be "increasingly at the controls," and we're not talking the driver's seat in the kids' car pool. That's right! Instead of just doing all the work outright, we'll be assigning it to ourselves first, then chewing ourselves out if we didn't get it done as soon as we said we should.

Franklin enjoys his favorite nature show; the fish, a little less

The series of articles on the future of working failed to take just one little detail into account. We are a nation of pet lovers. Our pets share our work places. The future of working is doomed.

Thanks to my exciting and rewarding career as a part-time newspaper reporter, I have enjoyed a sneak preview of the future *Time* so boldly predicts. Grab a hankie, and pull up a seat.

It is 5 a.m. and my boss, Bob, calls me in early to let her and Franklin out. As I pass Molly's cage on my way in to the office, the guinea pig chirps loudly for her lettuce. I stop at the 'fridge to pinch off a leaf, then tickle her belly as she stretches up to haul it into her cage.

I know it's sexual harassment, but she can't reach the phone to contact Legal.

I fill the two cat dishes and greet Callie, Employee of Every Month because the dog is the only one in the office who has any manners, me included. Then Bob scratches to get back in, where she buries her head in her food bowl. Franklin stays outside, dawdling as usual in the men's room.

I grab a coffee and head for my office. Six sentences into my workday, Franklin starts pawing at my window to get back in. He bounces from my chair to the floor, leaving snowy footprints on my seat, size XL because he has extra toes. Distracted by the traffic, I sit in the snow on my chair.

The time clock hasn't registered a full hour before Franklin starts an argument with Bob over who gets the best cubicle (spot in the sun). The fur flies. Callie hides under the coffee table. I leave my job to mediate with a well-aimed slipper.

Detecting movement in the room, Molly chirps for more lettuce. Franklin finally settles into his work routine, a cat nap on the couch, while Bob, clearly management, lies on her back on the kitchen floor and meows if another employee comes too close. Callie sighs at my knee.

What was I writing in the first place?

I hope this explains some of the work that I do, and I'm sorry it came in a little late. Franklin clipped my keyboard on his way in this morning, and then I was involved in a personal injury accident-- stepped on Bob's tail in the hallway.

Welcome to the future of working. It's a jungle in here.

Dogs Show Me Up

If you are a lover of all things dog, there was no better place to be awhile back than the Marquette Kennel Club's Annual Dog Show in Marquette.

From an easygoing Irish Wolfhound that fairly filled his pen to a little Chinese Crested that seriously needs a new look, the dogs went all out to entertain. And their owners didn't do too shabbily, either.

I hadn't been to a dog show since my college days, when I snapped off a quick assignment for Photography 101. Then I was unjustly downgraded for obviously missing the mark: the people in my photos looked just like their dogs.

A long-faced woman was pictured grooming her collie. A lady with a tight perm accessorized with her toy poodle, and a man who clearly had a rap sheet a mile long was captured on film, trotting his Bullmastiff around the ring.

Pardon me for being judgy. I learned it in Photography 101.

Years later, I am happy to report that dog shows are just as much fun and even less stressful, because I don't get graded anymore. I had a fine time at the show, snapped a few photos just to prove I still can, and came home with an even greater appreciation for dog owners of all breeds.

I went because two friends, Dennis and Diane, are club members and were working at the event. Two other friends, Mack and Sue, also like dogs and wanted to see Dennis and Diane in action. It cost just $4 per carload, and Mack was popping for lunch. I love dogs, my friends, and free meals!

The Marquette County Fairgrounds were filled with RV's, dog paraphernalia and plenty of people, too. We zeroed right in on Dennis, who was sporting a very natty suit and checking-in registrants. We complimented him on being well groomed. I think he growled at us.

So, we turned our attention instead to the stars of the show, in all shapes and sizes with matching owners. I admired the fact that the dogs had better hair than me, except for the Chinese Crested, and I admired their owners even more because they so obviously loved their breeds.

We visited with a woman showing her 9-year-old Hungarian Puli. The sheep herding breed originated over a thousand years ago, and has a heavy coat that hangs just like dreadlocks. Hers was the only Puli in the show that weekend. She was anticipating a strong finish.

Then there was the Keeshond lady. Her dog's name is Jack Daniels, and he's a class act, just like the whiskey. She said he's like her child, only better, because he behaves both in and out of the ring. She even had a story to prove it.

She and Jack were checking into a hotel one day, when she was told there would be an added fee for her dog. A family behind them included several children who had obviously flunked obedience training. She asked the manager if they had to pay more for their kids. Of course not!

So, she cut a deal. Both she and the family were checking-in for the weekend. At check-out, if Housekeeping found the family's room was cleaner, she'd gladly pay extra for her dog. If her room was cleaner, Jack Daniels would get a free ride.

Two days later, the hotel manager glumly admitted, "I owe ya' some money."

We traveled the Fairgrounds, meeting and admiring the best of breeds and people. We saw Diane in action, too, as she directed traffic in a show ring. When we complimented her on her nice outfit, she just smiled.

I wanted a hot dog at the show because that would be so ironic, but Mack made me sit and eat in town. If you get a chance next year, try to catch the show! Just don't cut any lodging deals involving a Keeshond named Jack Daniels, especially if the kiddies are acting up.

"Blackie" Rises Again

A very sad thing happened in Wausau, WI on Good Friday. A fish died.

I got the call the next day. Mom had a catch in her voice, and was hesitant to break the news to me over the phone. As an ace reporter (nagging daughter), I finally dragged it out of her.

"I couldn't tell you yesterday, because I was too upset," Mom said. "Blackie died."

For the record, it is not uncommon for fish to die on Fridays in Wisconsin. There are a lot of Catholics in the Badger State, and their rule book calls for meatless Fridays during Lent, which spans the 40 days preceding Easter.

Blessedly, many parishes rise to the call for sacrifice with delicious fish fries that pad both church coffers and their parishioners. Just recently, a Wausau woman bragged to me that, "Red Lobster is afraid to come in, because they can't compete with our parish fish fries!"

But we are not talking about any old walleye, perch or baked cod with a side of slaw and French fries. We are talking about the cherished pet that peered through its glass bowl on Mom's kitchen table and regularly witnessed her slaughtering me at Rummikub and Scrabble.

I knew Blackie was judging me. I could read it in his bubbles.

When Mom fed Blackie a pinch of food each day, she tapped his bowl first, then marveled at how he surfaced to eat. Actually, her tap created a small tsunami in Blackie's one-liter kingdom, and he was just riding out the waves. (By the way, "tsunami" is a seven-letter word. Fifty Scrabble points for Nancy!).

If I appear somewhat inured to my mother's grief, allow me to explain. Back when I was about eight years old, Mom didn't come clean with me about Goldie.

Goldie was one of a school of goldfish that took turns occupying the filmy fish bowl in our living room. Previous occupants included Goldie, Goldie and the unforgettable Goldie. One day I came home from school and noticed the current Goldie was missing. Mom was ready with the perfect alibi.

"She got one of those little blue stones caught in her throat, and we took her to the vet," said Mom, who just didn't have the energy that day to deal with third grade grief. "She's recovering."

"Nu-uh!" I cried. "She's dead, and you're just saying that!"

"No, she's not," Mom calmly replied. "The operation was a success, and the vet is keeping her until her throat feels better."

Well, now it made sense. Three days later, when Mom needed something from the dime store, Goldie was released from the hospital with a clean bill of health. The procedure must have been rough, though, because she came home with bigger eyes, a nicked tail, and a couple black spots--probably from the shots.

I shared the memory with Mom in an effort to ease her grief, and she of course denied it. A few days later, brother Mark offered his shabby condolences by asking if she had frozen Blackie's remains, and if so, was there any beer batter in the house?

Brothers can be so callous, which also has seven letters--another 50 Scrabble points for Nancy!

If I appear as callous as Mark, it is simply because while our mom works to sustain fish life, for the past two months I have dedicated my days to killing as many fish as I can. I do it with an ice auger, a hand line, fishing buddies Barry Drue or Tom Kruse and of course, my official Michigan DNR fishing license.

The killing spree begins with tip-ups on inland lakes. Then Keweenaw Bay freezes over, and it's time to move out onto Lake Superior. We drill two windows of opportunity through the ice, and I try to lure fish in with my "Jig Dance of Death." And do you know where all that murderous activity gets me?

If Blackie had truly wanted to live, he'd have ridden that tsunami right across state lines into Keweenaw Bay. We've put a small dent in the local lake trout population, but the fish aren't dying to take my bait. I can only assume they all have small stones lodged in their throats.

I offered up that story as a comfort to my mom, but she wasn't taking the bait, either. I blame Mark. But Mom's dear neighbor and traveling companion, Lee, knew just what to do in Mom's time of need.

She went to the vet and brought the patient home.

On a recent visit to Wausau, I was happy to find the fish bowl was back on the kitchen table and fully loaded. Lee had left Mom a note, "Hope you like your new fish!", and another Blackie that was now ogling me from inside his new surroundings, clearly bubbling, "Loser!"

Mom is in love again. Mark is still on probation. I'm going fishing at St. Michael's this Friday.

3. MIXED BAG

Asteroid Alert

If you are like me, it's a secret you'll want to keep. Also, you were mightily relieved to learn last week that 30 years from now, Asteroid 1997 XF11 is not going to drop out of the sky and bonk us on our heads.

The startling announcement was made scarcely 24 hours after the International Astronomical Union informed us that on Oct. 26, 2028, you wouldn't want to look up. However, both the content and source of this short-lived foreboding raised some important questions that still bear addressing, such as:

1. What kind of options do you get with an Asteroid 1997 XF11, and

2. Do you think the Astronomical Union holds its annual company picnic in the dark?

It's easy for us to be flippant about this moot issue, and I can't get the image of Chicken Little out of my head, though I wouldn't dream of burdening anyone else with it (he's cute and yellow and slightly daft). But what was it all about, and are we truly safe from that great big apple, I mean asteroid, in the sky?

According to my source, which is unfortunately datelined "Washington" and therefore loses some major credibility, the asteroid was first spotted by the University of Arizona Spacewatch program, and became asteroid no. 169 on its list of "potentially hazardous objects."

I liked that. To a mother, hazardous objects are hot dogs not cut into small pieces, and the scissors you're running with. Astronomers get the bigger picture, and this time they had it in detail, pegging the asteroid as a mile-long hazardous object coming at us at the very irresponsible speed of 17,000 mph.

I heard the first warning over the radio, and wasn't overly concerned. A 30-year deadline for averting an attack by a rock seemed kind of generous to me, probably because I'm not an astronomer. But our little daughter took it to heart, providing me with a gripping account that night of the big asteroid threat.

It happened before, she gravely explained, millions of years ago, and made the dinosaurs go away. I am probably the closest thing to a dinosaur in her eyes, hence the warning. I calmed her fears by assuring her we'd shoot it down first, maybe with one of those bullet-spraying vehicles her little brother loves to draw.

Then wouldn't you know it, before our little artist could pencil-in his first burst of artillery, the astronomers shot him down with an update. Instead of the asteroid passing within 30,000 miles of earth's borders, the margin was widened to roughly 600,000 miles.

My daughter feels better about her mother's future now, and I'm kind of relieved our taxes won't be increased to cover the cost of that boy's asteroid zapper. But before you put away your hard hats, consider the following from astronomer David Morrison, who specializes in asteroids at NASA's Ames Research Center in California: It ain't over yet.

In the best tradition of good old science fiction flicks and that 1960s hit, *The Twilight Zone*, Morrison holds that, "The most likely warning period for something hitting the earth is still zero. The first you would know is when you felt the ground shake and saw the fireball coming up over the horizon."

Years ago, Morrison and a panel of other experts proposed the government fund a systematic look at the heavens to determine which asteroids and comets were most likely to get intimate with Earth. This would help prevent future celestial surprises that you'd otherwise just hear about on the street:

"Hold still a minute, Joe! Is it my imagination, or is that spot over the horizon a great big fi..."

As we all know, government is much too busy in courts these days to have time to give the nation a head's up in case space starts throwing rocks. Instead, take a word of advice from a mom who has had her share of averting disasters:

If you feel the earth move under your feet, for heaven's sake, drop the scissors!

Hacker Shares Helpful Hints

The big, wide world of the internet is virtually teeming with distractions. They include animal videos, foods I should avoid, recipes I can't, and hacks.

For the blessedly uninformed, stay that way. The internet will suck your life away. It is the real reason my piano now resides in the Baraga High School band room. I was too busy playing to learn how to play it.

But this is not about my many human failings. This is about all the wonderful things you can do while you are not practicing *Claire de Lune*, like cleaning your hairbrush with a dryer sheet, and using Chapstick to heal a paper cut.

Hacks are, by modern definition, "novel methods of increasing productivity and efficiency." They involve using regular household objects for unintended but often amusing purposes, like cleaning your toilet bowl with Coca-Cola.

How about erasing a scratch on a wood surface by rubbing it with a walnut? Or coating your buttons with clear nail polish so the thread won't unravel? And did you know that if the power goes out, you can put a crayon in a glass cup, light the end, and it will burn for hours?

Before continuing, I should probably type an official disclaimer to avoid messy litigation:

OFFICIAL DISCLAIMER: Don't do any of this.

Whew. That was close. As I was typing, there is no limit to the creative ways in which you can use average household products to burn your house down. Unless you thought first to fill the battery gap in your smoke detector with tin foil balls.

I read it right on the internet, and there was even a picture to prove it. If you have AAA batteries instead of AA, fill the gap with balled-up tinfoil and, as they like to say in Finnish circles, Viola! You can tell when the kids are lighting up their crayons again.

It is a real eye opener. Stuck in the snow? Put your car floor mats under your tires. Got a stripped screw? Use a wooden matchstick to fill in the space and "screw as normal."

Trust me, I couldn't make this stuff up if I tried.

Use a can opener on tough plastic packaging. Stretch tight shoes by putting a bag of water in each, then putting them in a freezer overnight. Got a problem with pulling too far into your garage? Hang a tennis ball from the ceiling to bump your windshield before you hit your back wall.

Those are so helpful, it's not even funny. So, let's just shoot straight to my favorite, which is using your head to increase the range of your key fob.

We've all been there before. You exit the mall, and press your key fob to locate your vehicle. Then you press it harder, accompanied by profuse swearing. Then you realize you caught a ride to the mall with a friend.

If you drove yourself, hackers advise you use your head, holding the key fob up to your chin and opening your mouth wide while pressing the button. It supposedly increases its range, while decreasing traffic around you due to your disturbing behavior in the mall parking lot.

"It's science!" the internet assures us. "Your head acts as an antenna, and your brain's 80 percent water acts as a conductor."

OFFICIAL DISCLAIMER—Writer not responsible if reader pushes red "alarm" button instead.

Pinata Down!

The horse was down, yet the child continued to beat it with a stick.

"Its head is broke," hollered another youngster. "Keep hitting it on the head!"

"Me hit! Me hit!" screamed a toddler, jumping up and down in excitement.

I interrupt this disturbing scene to assure the reader that no animals or children were maimed or killed in the typing of this column. The horse was a pinata, and the kiddies just wanted to spill its guts so they could tank up on the candy inside.

Pinata parties are as old as the hills, or more specifically, the sixteenth century. Friars allegedly used pinatas to teach people about Christianity by designing them like a star, with seven hollow points to represent the seven deadly sins.

They are, not necessarily in order of deadliness, pride, greed, wrath, gluttony, lust, envy and sloth.

The star was hung overhead and the people took turns whacking it with a stick, busting off the points to symbolically conquer the sins, until it rained down their heavenly reward of processed sugar. And it only took three deadly sins—gluttony, greed, and wrath—to get the job done.

Five centuries later, pinata partiers have come a long way. Instead of taking the moral high road, we pick our pinatas to reflect a currently popular theme. For your littlest Christians' birthday parties, a unicorn pretty much covers all the bases.

Unicorns are magical creatures that can make adults fork over $10 for a stuffed horse with a horn. For twice as much, you can purchase a unicorn pinata that was specifically made to be unstuffed, and you still have to pay the price to fill its belly with candy.

There is just one little problem with your modern day pinata. Unlike pinatas of yore, which were made of pottery, pinatas nowadays are made of heavy-duty cardboard that is so strong it could have floated the Titanic.

Of course, none of that is evident to your modern consumer shopping for a children's party pinata. All the adult sees is an overpriced rainbow-hued horse with a horn. And you still have to fill its middle with all those heavenly rewards.

Once the horse has been fed, the fun can begin. An adult with long arms and a low I.Q. is typically engaged to hold the pinata aloft, dangling it from a broom handle. A blindfolded child is armed with a stick, spun around, then told to break the pinata, which long-arm is now gaily bobbing up and down.

It's a swing and a miss! Strike two, and the bobbing unicorn remains unscathed, incurring the second deadly sin of wrath. The jeers of sugar-deprived partygoers reach a fevered pitch as the youngster leaps up and nails the adult right in the breadbasket, causing both handler and horse to hit the deck.

The cardboard unicorn doesn't crack. It doesn't even dent. At this point, a second responsible parent steps in to decapitate the pinata, which sounds horrifying but is really a Christian act, especially if there is chocolate therein.

I naturally grab for the dark pieces, right after I've managed to catch my breath.

Pronunciation Primer

Imagine, if you will, my horror at learning that I've spent most of my life mispronouncing "Adirondack."

Can't imagine it? Try taking a stab at pronouncing the sea shell called a "conch."

If you said it the way it's spelled, you are a real conch head! Pull up

You say Adirondack, I say Adironback--we can both agree that they're cheap lawn chairs

an Adiron*Back* chair with me, and read about how wrong we are when we think we're speaking right.

According to Merriam Webster, we are all conch heads, correctly pronounced "conk heads." In fact, Merriam has compiled a long list of words we Americans slaughter on a daily basis. And it's all because of our ancestors.

Apparently, at least if you are Merriam, English boasts the hardest spelling of any Western language. This is because of the "mongrel" nature of our language, which occurred when an Anglo-Saxon, a Latin, an Old Norse and an Anglo French collectively jumped the fence.

They got to talking, then some joker started writing it all down. Before you knew it, Americans everywhere were failing their spelling tests because of letters that had no business being in words, like "solder."

If English made any sense, "solder" would appear on Realtors' signs outside houses that had just been sold. Instead, it is a low-melting alloy you heat to join other metals, usually after several tries and many d---s, which also boast a silent letter, just like the "l" in solder.

Did you learn to read from a primer? If you just hit the letter "i" with a mallet, you learned to read off a paint can! The correct pronunciation for the little book is "primmer", which actually sounds a whole lot "dumber."

That is the problem with getting it right when everybody else is getting it wrong. You stick out like a waistcoat in a world of torn tee shirts.

A waistcoat was something guys wore to look really hot in the 1600s, kind of like your present day torn tee shirt. They were basically vests, and they were pronounced "WES-kits," which looks nothing like the actual word.

This word struck a personal chord because, fast way forward to the 1970s, my Maria High School uniform consisted of a sensible skirt, a top and a weskit. And the nuns spelled it just like that. And I never thought to call them out on it, because they were nuns and I was a dumb freshman in a waistcoat.

There are no do-overs in the real world, which is why you should always mind your p's and q's but especially your p's when buying clapboard.

Did you just say "clap board?"

You weskit-wearer! The correct pronunciation is "KLAB-erd," as in, "He teased me about learning to read from a primer, so I clapboard him."

The last word on Merriam's list of words we regularly slaughter is one that is not commonly used, probably because Merriam would catch wind of it and call us out. It's recondite, defined appropriately enough as "difficult for one of ordinary understanding to comprehend."

Most people emphasize the second syllable. Like a good Finn, whose language is just as guttural as our own, you need to hit the first one with a splitting maul, "REC-on-dite," to get your point across in perfect English.

I recondite end it here.

Calling Mr. President

If you are any kind of American and were able to draw in the station, then you, too, saw the start of the 2002 Winter Olympics. In case you are among the millions who fell asleep waiting to see who would finally light the torch, it was TV weatherman Al Roker.

Gotcha'! It was actually a bunch of U.S. hockey players who beat the Soviets back in 1980. Serves you right for napping while history was being made, in an opening ceremony co-starring every child in Utah who owns a pair of ice skates.

As I sit and wait for the Olympics Sarcasm Police to come and haul me off to jail, an arrest on ice that is being carefully choreographed even as I type, there is just one more Olympic image I would like to share: Did you catch that shot of President Bush talking on a U.S. athlete's cell phone?

Past presidents have shown their support, kind of, for Winter Olympics by sending a close facsimile thereof to attend the opening ceremonies. Presidential fill-ins have included vice presidents and other representatives who wanted to continue calling the president "boss."

In 2002, we got the real deal.

President George W. Bush made Olympic history by proclaiming the start of the games in person. Then he and his wife politely watched the Parade of Nations, though he did scowl rather fiercely at athletes from a country we are currently really mad at.

To his credit, and maybe because Laura was sitting next to him, he didn't roll his program into a megaphone and holler, "BOO!"

As I watched the athletes file into the stadium, proudly waving flags that were bigger than some of the countries they were representing, I couldn't help noticing the number of cell phones they were carrying, waving, and even talking into.

You're in Utah, for crying out loud. Who ya' gonna' call?

- "Hi Mom! See me? I'm on my phone!"

- "Hello, Domino's? Do you deliver to the Olympic Village?"

- "Hey, Salt Lake City Drugs--you got Prince Albert in a can?"

When the athletes had all filed in, the camera found Bush again, this time in the very midst of the U.S. Olympic team. While the media reported on how amazing it was to see Bush there, him not being an Olympic athlete and all, a girl on the president's left suddenly thrust her cell phone to his head.

Secret Service men throughout the stadium were suddenly on high alert. Hesitant to interrupt a private call, they just stayed really alert. Then Bush smiled, obviously confirming the pizza order for Domino's, and the threat of cell phone terrorism was over.

Bush's brush with the phone reminded me of another U.S. president, one who did not get to the Winter Olympics but came close to being quoted in our very own hometown newspaper. On a slow news day in

1983, I personally called the White House to question President Ronald Reagan about a new trucking tax.

And the White House called me back.

I had already interviewed local truckers earlier that day about how the new tax would adversely impact them, and wondered aloud why the president had signed it into law. My editor, working nearby, distractedly noted it was cheaper to call out-of-state than to Lansing; why not just dial Ron direct?

If you can believe it, the White House was listed under "information," and before the noon whistle blew in L'Anse, I was talking to our Nation's Capital. The woman who answered the phone said the president was busy, but sometimes answered calls (by obscure reporters) at the end of the day.

I tucked into other assignments while waiting to hear back from the president. Closing time does not wait for world leaders, and neither does Nancy, so at promptly 5 p.m. I snapped my notepad shut, gave up on Reagan and went home.

Later that evening our publisher, Ed Danner, was sitting at his desk at work when the telephone rang. It was the White House calling me back, and after hearing about the exchange from Ed, I doubted the president would try again later.

"This is the White House. Is Nancy Besonen there?"

"The WHAT?"

"The White House. Nancy Besonen called earlier today."

"YOU'RE KIDDING!"

I have been writing about fishing ever since, when I'm not busy picking on American institutions like the Winter Olympics and Al Roker. But my heart was stirred by what I saw in Utah, and now I, too, harbor an Olympic-size dream.

It's another call, same idea, new administration, but this time I beat Ed to the phone.

"Hi, Nancy? This is the president. You had a question about some trucking tax?"

Prone From Accidents

There is a reason that accidents happen. It is because no one in their right mind would do such a thing on purpose.

The theory was upheld several winters ago when I watched in fascinated horror (universally accepted way of watching an accident happen) as a man reached barehanded into freezing water, grabbed a

40-inch northern pike by its razor-sharp gills, and hauled it onto the ice.

He suffered a small scratch. However, a short time later, the man who had caught the fish brushed his mitt against the business end of an ice auger. I didn't see that, but word on the lake was he'd cut his hand clear to the bone.

One man took a calculated risk. The other suffered a bona fide accident. Both became legends on the lake, especially after the angler opted to forego medical attention in favor of tightly-wrapped tape and a hearty swig of anesthesia.

We are all legends in our own minds, and in our medical records thanks to years of accidental living. The process begins when our minds are still developing. It accelerates some on our developmental downward slide.

Children do all sorts of accidental things on purpose. They walk under sharp overhangs with zero clearance (June 1966), run into barbed wire on a family picnic (July 1966) and let go of the handlebars while pedaling Kay McMillan's bike to see if they can stay upright (August 1966—met the deductible!).

In all fairness, other people's kids aren't so bright, either. Their noses get in the way of snow shovels. They ride their bicycles between two trees, and get caught by their ears. They try to teach an old dog new tricks, and the dog gives them more than the paw.

The worst part of taking your child to the ER is knowing that, shortly after arrival, you will be asked two embarrassing questions. First, how did your child's head get in the way of the merry-go-round, and second, when was your child's last tetanus shot?

Parents keep careful records. The problem is, some of us keep them on grocery lists, bank deposit receipts or calendars that are thrown away the following February, sometimes March. Our frequently vaccinated children are tetanus's worst enemy.

Adults are just as prone to accidents as children. That's because we are often acting like children when they happen, as in:

- the friend who burnt her nose trying to eat a melted chocolate chip off a hot cookie sheet, and

- the brother who broke his ankle showing his sons how he used to climb a stone monument in the park

- did I type "brother?" I meant "another" (it was Bobby)

Accidents are proof positive that there will always be a place in this world for people who act outside of their right minds. It's called the ER, or the walk-in clinic if you don't need stitches.

Having beaten the odds by reaching adulthood, I am proud to say I haven't visited an emergency room for at least the past five years. Unless I wind up in one tomorrow, in which case my last tetanus shot, I'm sure of it, was last year. The time before that was due to a selfless, downright heroic act: I saved my mom from an olive can.

It was the day after Thanksgiving, and Mom was using a butter knife to try and wedge the lid off a half-opened can of black olives.

"Give me that thing, before you hurt yourself," I said.

A moment later my sister-in-law, who earned her medical degree working in an elementary school office, advised, "It'll quit bleeding if your just squeeze your finger hard... squeeze it a little harder... OK, you might want to have that looked at."

To her credit, my sister-in-law's opinion was initially upheld by the ER nurse--"They don't usually put stitches in fingertips"—and then overruled by the doctor, who bent my finger and had to duck the flow. While he sewed, he commended me for apparently not being a smoker.

Mom was a real sport, too. Before we left for the hospital, Mark was digging an olive out of the now open can to sustain him during a long wait at the ER when she joked, "Watch out--there aren't supposed to be any pimentos in black olives!"

It is just that kind of compassion, plus the threat of a tetanus shot update, that keeps me from reaching into olive cans or the gills of oversize pike. I don't clean ice augers, either—unless the anesthesia is flowing freely.

4. WILD THINGS

Crop Adjuster Breaches Security

Dear State of Michigan,

I am writing regarding one of your whitetail deer, which you take great pride in owning and managing until it steps in front of our motor vehicle and then we should contact our insurance agency.

Your deer is eating our garden. You should raise your deer better. LIKE ON A RAILROAD TRACK!

Pardon my outburst. Gardening is my therapy, and my sessions grow shorter every day because your whitetail deer is visiting our garden every night, and our homeowner's insurance doesn't cover carrots.

The problem began last summer when a local doe developed a taste for domestic. Instead of shopping co-op, which would have solved the problem because it's on a busy highway and deer don't look both ways, she turned tail and hopped our garden fence.

I discovered the B&E—breaking & eating—the following day when I went outside for my morning therapy and encountered a row of headless green beans. It added years to my treatment. By way of retaliation, we added juice to our garden fence.

An electrified wire was run from our garage to the fence. The deer must have made the connection, because the midnight raids ended and peas were restored to the kingdom. We even got a few green beans out of a second planting.

We hoped the doe would die a dirty death, but last winter was mild and traffic has been light and your deer is now back at the bait pile of her dreams. And this time, we're having trouble turning her away.

We ran the wire again and I tested it with the back of my hand, jumping just high enough to assure my husband that shock therapy was working. Then we retired inside to watch one of our favorite TV shows, featuring people who shoot garden pests.

Late season apples are a hard sell for a young buck who preferred our garden

In the meantime, we couldn't wait for our guest to get her buzz on. And we're still waiting, because overnight, her B&E skills grew by leaps and bounds over our garden fence. The following morning our beets had been defoliated and three cabbages were MIA. This was war!

Unfortunately, we are sadly lacking in artillery. We can't amp up the electricity or we'll burn down the garage. We can't post a guard dog because we have a cat, and chasing deer is beneath Franklin's dignity.

Instead, we broke out the Wind Chime of Death.

The big chime ordinarily hangs in our living room, safely out of reach from both the wind and grandchildren. Its deafening ring could call the cows home from across state lines. To the doe's discerning ear, it was dinner music.

Plan B called for diminishing the dining experience by blocking access to the salad bar. I drove stakes into the ground between the vegetable rows, strung them with fishing line, then turned toward the house to eagerly await the floor show. As it turned out, I was the opening act.

My foot snagged the line as I spun, causing me to topple into the cucumber patch. As I struggled to untangle myself, the wind found the chime, which bonged an ear-splitting death knell overhead for the cukes that I was currently dispatching.

Somewhere in the woods behind me, I swear I heard the doe snicker.

My husband, who would rather eat deer than vegetables anyway, encourages me to abandon my therapy. The surviving plants would do better just fending for themselves, he said, hiding under our most abundant crop which is weeds.

The grandkids, who miss having the wind chime inside the house, would gladly forfeit all their vegetables to the deer, except for the garden carrots they like to wipe clean on Gummi's jeans while I'm scrambling in the cucumber patch.

In closing, I implore you to please manage your natural resource better and keep her out of my garden, or I will repay you with a personal delivery from our second most abundant crop, overgrown zucchinis.

Strangely enough, your deer won't touch them.

Hooked on Hunting

I read the headline, and was hooked like a herring: "We Fought a Blue Marlin for 22 ½ Hours and Lost Him."

It appeared in *Anglers Journal,* a magazine my editor and frequent fishing partner, Barry Drue, shares with me. I thank him by keeping the pretzel jar on my desk fully stocked at all times, because he'd just use my *Better Homes & Gardens* to clean his fish.

There are a lot of misguided anglers out there who care more about the fight than the filets. If you listen carefully, you can actually hear their voices rise in heated response to my well-aimed dig:

"Huh?"

Okay, so maybe I'm not the rabble rouser I think I am, but people tend to have strong opinions about fishing. Some swear by light line and tackle for a fair fight. The rest of us like to play it safe with gear so stout the fish can barely take it all in.

Unless they are a blue marlin.

The boat that hooked the one that got away was loaded for bear, but latched onto a behemoth. Its crew fought the mighty blue marlin from 10 a.m. to 8:30 a.m. *the following day,* running out of food, water and luck before the big one finally got away.

That is the problem with playing a fish. The longer it goes on, the greater the chance you will star in a humbling article in *Angler's Journal.* Worse yet, you can lose your fish. But you can still hold your head high, because you did it in a sporting manner.

A few years back at Fish Camp, which is like your U.P. Deer Camp only slightly smellier, a man sitting beside me at the lodge bar said he once landed a 45-inch musky on four-pound test fishing line. I responded by changing my seat.

He adjusted his volume accordingly, and proceeded to preach a full sermon on adjusting your drag and playing the fish out until it surrenders, exhausted, at the side of your boat. Then, being a true sportsman, you let it go.

I left before he could pass the collection plate, still feeling the sting from having my 10-pound test parted that very morning, possibly by a feisty bluegill. I should have used heavy braided.

If you are wondering where I am going with this, well, so am I. The most likely direction is, how do deer hunters manage to dodge the sporting bullet?

There is no catch & release in the woods. It is dispatch & devour, or if you're really successful, shoot & stuff. Hunters have to track their prey, just like fishermen, but they aren't expected to use light artillery when they finally catch up to it.

A few years back, I proposed a Paint Ball Buck Hunting season. Instead of having to buy bullets, hunters would be issued hues, then set loose in the woods to paintball their bucks in Ravishing Red, Coral Craze, Vibrant Violet, etc.

Yeah, still waiting to get a bite on that one. In the meantime, I've got another big idea in the hopper, inspired by both catch & release and my usual form of literary entertainment, which is Louis L'Amour Western novels: Buck Roping!

Instead of shooting your prey, a privilege we fishermen lost long ago because musky anglers were blowing holes in their boats and going down with their fish, you'd have to "dab a loop on that bronc" (channeling Louis here), then hang on for the ride.

I can see it now, deer rocketing through the woods, hauling their hunters behind them. Still more would be trailing their lassos, liberated by having won what is finally a fair fight. Best of all, I could finally join the ranks of true sportsmen everywhere, and share my own battle in print:

"I Fought a Spike Horn for 22 ½ Hours and Lost Him."

'Twas the Second Week of Deer Camp

(With sincere apologies to Clement Clarke Moore,
author of *A Visit From St. Nicholas*)
(and to Santa Claus, or "Heikki Lunta" in Finn)

'Twas the second week of deer camp, and all through the house,
Not a creature was stirring, we'd killed the camp mouse
The stockings were hung by the heater with care
Which explained the foul smell permeating the air

The hunters were nestled all snug in their beds
While visions of big bucks danced through their sore heads
I checked on the fire and hung up my chook
And had just settled down with the Hunting Rule Book

When out on the roof there arose such a fuss
I thought it would cave in and heap snow on us
Away to the window I flew like The Flash
Leaving a trail through a week's worth of trash

The moon that shone bright on the new-fallen snow
Cast unfortunate light on our camp down below
When what to my bleary red eyes should appear
But a hay wagon pulled by eight whitetail deer

With a man whistling a song I didn't know the tune ta'
I knew in a moment—it's old Heikki Lunta!
More rapid than winter his big bucks they came
And he whistled and shouted, and called them by name

"Now Vernor! Now Victor!
Now Toivo! Now Reino!
On Axel! On August!
On Helmer and Aino!

"To the top of the deck
To the top of this camp
Skip the steps, boys,
Use that snow for a ramp!"

As empty cans by the November gales fly
When the piles get so high, they mount up to the sky
So up to our camp roof the whitetails they flew
With a sleigh of supplies and that old Heikki too

In the span of three loud snores, I heard on the roof
The prance and the paw of each impatient hoof
I turned from the window and ran to the fire
But I was too late—Heikki'd singed his attire

He was dressed all in camo, from head to his foot
His coveralls covered in ashes and soot
A bundle of goodies flung onto his back
Like a whole sporting section squeezed into one pack

Hunting knives, how they glinted! A camp stove, how merry!
Blaze orange everything, sizes may vary
A fresh stock of jerky, for many a meal
An untouched deer decoy—this buck's got appeal!

Gloves for deer gutting, a rope for transporting
A scale for weighing, a mount kit, how sporting!
He looked 'round our camp which was really quite smelly
And added Glade Air Freshener—Christmas Mint Jelly

He was chubby and plump, like a good deer camp cook
And I laughed when I saw him, and he gave me a look
And a wink, that old sass, then grabbing a beer
He rose up the chimney and back to his deer

He sprung to his seat, to his team gave a whistle
Seeing bucks fly away made my back kind of bristle
But I heard him exclaim as he drove out of sight
"Happy hunting to all—and your camp is a fright!"

Deer With a Difference

"Sic 'em, Palm!"

Our little mutt raced across the field at a doe feeding on the hill. The deer eyed the black-and-white missile hurtling toward her until he skidded to a stop, right under her chin. Then she dealt his ego a fatal blow by stamping her foot in irritation and resuming her meal.

Palmer sulked back to the house, where he now spends his days just flipping around mice the cat killed. It's going to take years of pats on the head and reminders that he still has a great personality before old Palm is once again the dog he was, whatever that was.

I'm not typing this so Palmer's buddies and the cat can rub his whiskers in it. Instead, I'm giving fair warning to our visiting hunters, who help support our fair peninsula with their purchases of snacks and tasty beverages and gear to replace what they left on their garage floors.

There's something a little different about the deer this year.

Whitetail deer are by nature a delicate, retiring species that feed at dawn and dusk, hiding during the day to digest their food and excusing themselves after every burp. They raise their tails like flags in times of distress to alert others, and then they go hide again.

This is the species I remember from my youth. On vacations to Mercer, WI, when the cabin our folks rented on Fisher Lake grew too small at night, they'd trundle my three brothers and me into the car and cruise country roads in search of whitetail deer.

We thrilled at the sight of eyes glowing through the dark woods as the deer hid from predators and kid-filled cars, and then we fell asleep. Now fully grown and wide awake, especially when driving in the ruminant-riddled U.P., I would like to know where all those nice deer went.

Whitetails today display a different behavior pattern. It's called "attitude." They eat whenever and wherever they want, preferably with an unobstructed view of heavy traffic.

Instead of spending their days in hiding, they masquerade as lawn ornaments, or strike DNR decoy poses and try not to blink as cars slowly pass by. Then all of a sudden, some joker breaks rank and makes a run for the center line, causing statewide car insurance rates to go up another nickel.

U.P. drivers adjust accordingly. We lean forward in our seats while driving, to better see what we're about to hit. We tap our brakes at anything that glows in the dark. We save up all our nickels. For all that and more, we still get shortchanged by whitetail deer, who only go off-road to raid our gardens.

And quite frankly, I don't know how they can tell the difference.

Michigan's state plant is a rock. Frost heaves up a fresh batch every spring. We have to pick before we can plant. When we finally succeed in teasing a few sprouts up between the rocks we missed, the deer jump both Palmer and the fence.

They took the leap this year on a warm night in July, when Palmer was dreaming of his self-respect and there wasn't enough traffic to keep the deer interested in roadside dining. As usual, our sense of security took a worse hit than our pitiful produce. You just never knew when those punks were going to strike again, flashing their tails like gang signs as they merged back into traffic.

The final insult is that all the havoc is being wreaked by does and fawns, which are both above the law. As hunting season nears, bucks invariably go into hiding, keeping a low profile while awaiting the take-out order they gave mom and the kids before they left for their nightly garden raid:

"A buncha' beets, and some of them carrots she hasn't gotten around to digging up yet. I'll meet ya' alongside M-28. Oh, and snort at that little dog for me on the way out, willya'? Heh heh heh!"

Talking Turkey

With bird hunting season coming into full swing (duck, goose, ruffed grouse, rotisserie chicken if you miss), let us pause a moment to reflect upon one that won't be ducking: the bald eagle.

The biggest bird of prey occurs throughout the U.S., in most of Canada and Alaska and even a little bit of Mexico. And like a good Yooper, it is found near large bodies of open water with an abundant supply of fish and game.

In 1782, the bald eagle literally dodged the bullet by successfully campaigning to become both our national bird and animal, thereby doubling its insurance against ever coming under fire from its kinsmen. Two years later, Benjamin Franklin famously bemoaned the fact the turkey had lost the vote.

Franklin said it all in a letter he wrote to his daughter after the eagle had landed its plum assignment. It's kind of harsh--who knew Ben was such a bird basher?--but he bases his case on hard facts about our national bird/animal, such as, it's kind of opportunistic:

"*...he watches the Labour of the Fishing Hawk; and when that diligent Bird has at length taken a Fish, and is bearing it to his Nest for the Support of his Mate and young Ones, the Bald Eagle pursues it and takes it from him.*"

Don't you love how people used to talk? The capitalization is a bit dodgy; it had my computer blowing chips, but I'd appreciate being recognized now and then for the Labour of my Fishing, which I bear to my Nest for the Support of my Mate.

Back to the proud bird, I have seen its opportunism with my own eyes. Actually, I heard it with my own ears, because I was below decks slapping sandwiches together on the proud *Miss Laurie* for myself, Cap'n John, Barry and my husband, Don, when the cowardly bald eagle struck.

I had caught a lake trout that was so small my fishing partners wouldn't even run for the ruler, which was still wet from my last undersize catch. I slipped it over the side of the boat to dive back for the deep. Then I did the same, heading below to hunt up some grub for our lunch, when I suddenly heard raucous squawking overhead.

We had guests! Actually, it was just a bunch of seagulls, arguing over my fish that obviously shared my poor sense of direction because it headed due north instead of south. Then I heard something about an eagle, followed by loud whoops and more squawks, and a moment of silence.

It was for my fish, now being ferried aloft by our national bird which had flown out from shore and stolen it from the seagulls. We considered saluting as it beat its retreat, but because we, too, are opportunistic eaters, we wolfed down our ham on wheat sandwiches while continuing to jig for bigger fish.

We could have been enjoying bald eagle on rye, if the vote had only gone the other way. It seems that way back then, Congress was all about anything Roman. Actually, it was impressed by the Roman Republic, which decorated heavily in bald eagle, which didn't impress Benjamin one bit:

"*For in Truth the Turkey is in Comparison a much more respectable Bird, and withal a true original Native of America. He is besides, though a little vain & silly, a Bird of Courage and would not hesitate to attack a Grenadier of the British Guards who should presume to invade his Farm Yard with a red Coat on.*"

I am totally Team Ben on this one, because I was once a mother of small children who wandered too close to a turkey while visiting a petting zoo with their Aunt Joan. I don't think the kids were wearing red coats, but the turkey attacked them anyway.

Luckily for them, Aunt Joan walked softly but carried a monstrous purse. She flung it in the dirt at the turkey's feet, causing the Bird of Courage to gobble in disgust and go looking for children who didn't bring their heavily armed aunt along to the petting zoo.

Luckily for the U.S., the proud bird won the vote, because if you think about it, our world would be a much different place if bald eagles were on the radar. And so would our own Baraga County.

We'd have the Fraternal Order of Turkeys Club on U.S. 41 in L'Anse. We'd be taking pride in our former L'Anse Turkeys Drum & Bugle Corps. Worse yet, our Ottawa Sportsmen's Club in Pelkie would host an annual Bald Eagle Shoot.

In spite of it all, we as Americans can fully appreciate Ben's foresight in this very trying presidential election year. If he'd just managed to swing that vote, when our new president stepped off Air Force One we could have proudly honored him/her with a big, resounding:

"The Turkey has landed!"

5. REEL ME IN

Digging Up Bones

I was warming a pew before Sunday School when a youngster seated behind me asked the inevitable.

"Been huntin'?"

"Went and done," I proudly replied.

"How big?"

"Uh, spikehorn."

The corner of his mouth twitched, then he smiled wide and ran off to rat me out to his little buddies. That's when I knew he'd just been downgraded from a King of Orient Are to a hairy shepherd in this year's Sunday School Christmas Pageant.

Just kidding! I would never pick on an innocent child. Besides, he's also pegged for a *Friendly Beast* solo, because even though he aims a little high at deer hunting, the boy's got pipes.

The story is the same every deer season. I sit in my blind, rattling in my buck with two no. 2 pencils. Something young and tender arrives, and is promptly dispatched. I happily notch another hunting license, one point on each side.

And I officially become a target.

There is no arguing that antlers are important. They help deer decide who gets a date. They help successful hunters get a grip while dragging their prize from the woods. They are the ultimate Northwoods accent piece, suitable for hanging in any room, but mostly ones frequented by Northwoods men.

Everyone wants a big buck. I want one, too, but they seldom walk in front of my gun. And do you know what is ironic? The opposite of what is expected. Also, holding out for an old swamp buck when you could be enjoying veal.

Would you go to a restaurant and order the oldest, toughest steak in the house? I think not! But as long as my fellow hunters have me in their sights and are tugging at the trigger, I may as well bait my fellow fishermen, too.

I like spikes and I fish for pikes.

I know pike is already plural, but Spell checker allowed it because it thinks I am typing about a long weapon with a pointed head. And Spell checker is not that far from the truth, because northern pike have long bodies and pointy heads.

They are also slimy and have bad dispositions. And those are their good points.

Pike are chock-full of Y-shaped bones that make them hard to filet, and even harder to eat. That is the main reason most people don't fish for them, or gingerly throw them back if they accidentally hook one, taking care not to get hooked in the process by their razor-sharp teeth.

You want irony? People don't like fish that are bony, but they love barbecued ribs and chicken wings!

My Finnish father-in-law, who enjoyed many a bowlful of kala mojakka (fish head stew) in his day, liked to tell the story of an old Finlander who popped pike into one side of his mouth, and spat the bones out the other side.

I prefer to get most of the bones out with my filet knife in the fish cleaning shack. I use my fork to remove the rest from the roof of my mouth—kind of like a hairy shepherd who has a taste for veal.

Write a Winning Fish Tale

With the deadline for our newspaper's annual Fish Tales Contest fast approaching, I am compelled to remind readers it is time to actually write your stories.

Then you need to mail them to me to be in the running for this year's fabulous Fish Tales prizes! They include the Kanger Survival and Fishing Tool for Venture, a keychain shaped like a little spinning reel, an authentic Goofy bobber, and a size XL tee shirt proclaiming, "Women Love Me, Fish Fear Me."

Of course, it is easy for me to make literary demands upon my readers because I hold a literary degree. I hold it at least several times a year, when I have to dig under my college diploma to retrieve something I need from our drawer of random documents.

Also, I spend a fair amount of time writing.

The hardest thing about writing is finding a pen that works. The second hardest thing about writing is deciding how to begin your story, because it will literally make or break your Fish Tale.

I do not encourage cheating. I do encourage outright bribery, but nobody seems to be listening to that rule, either. Therefore, I am figuratively tossing the rule book out the window by offering the following gently-used openings for your otherwise 100 percent original Fish Tale:

- *Once upon a time...*
- *It was a dark and stormy night...*
- *Call me Ishmael.*

If option number three sounds vaguely familiar, it is because I lifted it from the biggest fish tale of all time, Herman Melville's classic, "Moby Dick" starring Gregory Peck. It is all about a crazy boat captain's pursuit of a great white whale. For a local angle, you might want to substitute a whitefish.

As a matter of fact, writers who choose to open their Fish Tale with number three may be in direct violation of copyright laws, in which case the Kanger Survival and Fishing Tool for Venture, with 11 special attachments and its own leatherette case, would serve them well while doing hard time.

Once you have your opening line, the rest of your Fish Tale should flow like Sturgeon River in the springtime, until you hit a logjam, like a Fish Tales author-in-progress did just last week. The following is a factual transcript (best recollection) of her call of distress:

"Hello, is this Nancy?"

"Yup."

"How do you spell 'lunker'?"

I talked her through the crisis, keeping her on the line until she found a working pen and then making her repeat the spelling because I was on the clock. Then she hung up on me so she could finish typing her Fish Tale.

The ability to flesh-out a Fish Tale with colorful vernacular can make all the difference between, say, winning a bobber and a keychain. For readers who do not have access to a literary degree or a Watton phone book, I'm offering up a few helpful hints.

A big fish is a lunker, a whopper, or with apologies to Melville, a "Mo' Dicker." Fish don't just take the bait. They shatter the surface to hit it like a freight train or explode from under a stump, then peel line off your reel so fast it sings, even if they are a perch.

You play the fish out, haul it in, then gun it for shore with your boat riding low under the weight of your trophy. Long after its last gasp, your fish will continue to grow in your memory and frequent recounting until it achieves "behemoth" proportions.

Congratulations! You're ready to write about fishing. Four prizes are available, but so long as the dollar store is open for business, no Fish Tale will go unrewarded. And if ending your tale should prove as challenging as starting it, allow me to suggest just two magic words that will guarantee its success: check enclosed.

Is Trout Worship Wrong?

We are two weeks into the Lenten season, and quite frankly, I am a bit concerned about my overall lack of suffering.

For time immemorial, I've given up candy for Lent. The sacrifice was suggested to me by a nun. There's a reason those women wear black.

It is a proven fact children have a biological need for Jolly Ranchers and Snickers bars. The data, you ask? All right, then, you have caught me in a boldface lie. But I didn't give up lying for Lent, so HA HA HA!

In case you were never schooled by women in black, Lent is that period between Ash Wednesday and Easter when you don't want to cross a Catholic. We're encouraged to give up something near and dear to us to make us stronger in our faith. We might take it out on you.

In childhood, candy was about the biggest sacrifice I could make. For 40 days I couldn't squander my lunch money on candy, beg my friends for candy or ruin my dinner with candy. It was a life-altering experience. And each year, I failed miserably at it.

I was still blinking through the ashes falling off my forehead on Ash Wednesday when my resolve would start to waver. I didn't go straight from church to the candy store—in Chicago, nobody sells candy to a kid with a smudged forehead on Ash Wednesday—but I came close.

Someone would give me a candy bar, probably my equally corrupt but Protestant friend, Cheri, and I'd squirrel it away in my sock drawer. Then I'd need to change my socks, sometimes that very same day. I'd take a little nibble, just to test the faith. Then I'd fail the test.

Early on, my Lenten suffering was not borne of sacrifice, but of guilt. And that is no small matter, because in the Catholic faith, guilt kills. Jesus died for my sins. I cannot go two days without a Kit Kat bar. I am going for the eternal burn.

After 40-some years of doing a slow simmer during Lent, I have finally mastered the technique. I outgrew my dependence upon candy. I still hold it close to my heart, and even closer to my hips, but I can do 40 days of no candy without breaking a low sugar sweat.

That could be an indication I should change it up and move onto another form of personal sacrifice during Lent, but I choose to ignore it. If I listened to the little guardian angel perched on my shoulder, I might give up something even closer to my heart. Like ice fishing.

During ice fishing season on Lake Superior's Keweenaw Bay, I have a problem with lake trout. Actually, my friend Barry does. He suffers from an addiction. Armed with sucker bait, my ice tent and my ol' pal, Mr. Heater, I am his enabler.

If an opportunity to fish should arise, even if we have to create it, we will walk out onto the bay, pitch our tent, drop a line about 260 feet down and be fishers of lake trout. Doesn't that sound kind of Biblical to you? Me too! And that was my excuse for missing Sunday School last week.

Actually, I had a reporting assignment in town, covering TV6 Weatherman Karl Bohnak's visit to the L'Anse Library Open House. And I planned on hitting it, right after playing guitar for Sunday School. And then Barry called to ask, "Wanna' go fishing Sunday morning?"

I didn't recognize the threat to my Christianity because he wasn't offering me a Hershey bar, so I readily agreed. I left a message with the pastor's son, who blessedly did not question my reason for not being there to lead "Jesus' Love is a Bubblin' Over," and went fishing.

As it turned out, the lake trout were "bubblin' over!" We caught our limit by 11:30 a.m., and I was right on time for my assignment at the library. I arrived with a bad case of hat head and smelled rather fishy, but Karl was distracted by a storm on the horizon so he shook my hand, anyway.

And I didn't eat one candy bar out on the ice, or even think about chocolate while the fish were hitting, so I am thinking I'm in the clear here. I'll be back at Sunday School again next week, "Bubblin' Over" with the best of them.

Except in my case, the heat will be a little higher.

Fish Camp Goes Co-ed

Greetings!

Once again, in direct defiance of the United States Postcard System, I am saving roughly $1,416.31 writing our newspaper readers a Fish Camp report. I am even including a photo, so you can wrap more fish with it when you're done reading.

Mark and daughter Amanda catch up during a lazy day at Fish Camp

Fish Camp is, as always, an annual gathering at The Hideaway resort in Mercer, WI for questionable characters from Chicago's South Side. In the 1920s and '30s, the Northwoods was a favorite hangout for some of Chicago's most notorious gangsters, like Al Capone and John Dillinger.

It's since been taken over by The Boys.

The Boys are, in order of disorderly conduct, J.K., LeGear, Slick, and Mard. Mard was the best-behaved this year, only because he wasn't able to make it. Joelyn, his fiancé at last year's Fish Camp, is now his wife, and she knows bad influences when she has fished with them. Until Mard makes it back to Camp, Joelyn is pretty high up on The Boys' hit list.

Rounding out the gang are Mike, 17, Sam, 18, and H.B. Mike is my brother Slick's son, and Sam is mine. They are the heirs apparent to

The Boys' legacy of hard fishing on the Turtle Flambeau Flowage, raucous pool playing at The Hideaway lodge at night, and sleeping in until most of the fish are done with their breakfasts. As for H.B., that would be me.

I will not tell you what H.B. stands for, because impressionable children might be reading, but I can say I got my nickname by cleaning up at Fish Camp. During my first stay, I kicked a path through the beer cans and swiped a couple days' accumulation of bacon grease off the stove. And that's all it took--I've been a bad word ever since.

If The Boys thought that was bad, they must have been quivering in their mildewy socks (The Boys never bail their boats) this year, as two more women were scheduled to come to Camp: Slick's wife, Joan, and their daughter, Amanda. Both came to see what the big deal was about Fish Camp.

Joan bathes regularly and does not fish. She has lovely skin which she protects with liberal applications of sunscreen before taking healthful rows on the Flowage. In comparison, H.B. looks like one of those leather change purses they sell at the Wampum Shop in Mercer. And my socks are a bit damp, too.

Amanda, age 20, was casting like a pro after only one short tutorial on the dock. We fished together over miles of still water, then paddle boated through whitecaps. Taking her cue from Mike and Sam, she bought and gamely dispatched a watermelon-flavored cigar that gagged every mosquito in her air space. Its green case is my official souvenir from this year's Fish Camp.

When Slick first learned his womenfolk would be joining us, he welcomed them with a snarl: "We ain't gonna' turn this into some family thing!" The day after Joan arrived, J.K. was guiding a leering Slick away from the girls' cabin, warning, "We ain't havin' none of that 'koochie koo' here!"

The Boys survived The Girls and even enjoyed their company, though the women drew the line at gulping a live tadpole, a hallowed Fish Camp initiation rite. Cleaning was kept to a minimum--double lane paths between the beer cans-- and The Boys endured the occasional vegetable with their Fish Camp meals of grilled meat, side of meat and hot sauce.

Fishing was fair to middling for us, and excellent for folks who knew what they were doing. Slick raised a musky, the pride of the Northwoods, his first day out, but it spat the plug while J.K. was scrambling for the net. LeGear raised two muskies with this year's embarrassment from the Chicago Sportsmen's Show: the "Flub Dub."

The Flub Dub is a fluorescent orange torpedo of a lure with a spinner on its front and a treble hook dangling off the back. Flub Dubs are so stupid looking, muskies hit them just to get them off the lake.

The first musky was so insulted, it broke LeGear's line and sank back into the shallows, taking his Flub Dub with it. The second musky missed a larger Flub Dub, but probably suffered permanent eye damage from tracking its lurid path through the weeds. We teased LeGear mercilessly, and will shop accordingly for a multiple Flub Dub assault on the Flowage next summer.

Of course, no Fish Camp is complete without some historical research conducted on hazy afternoons at the Local Bar (real name) in Mercer. The Boys met up there with an old-timer named Marv, who helped them track down Charles Comiskey's former camp site on the Flowage.

Comiskey owned the White Sox in the early 1900s, and built their home stadium, Comiskey Park, in Chicago. It was The Boys' favorite place of worship when they were growing up together in the city, and they're still devoted to the team that always seems to come in second to the Cubs, no matter what their standings.

As it turned out, the camp was a short hike away from our resort, though it nearly killed LeGear ("There is nothing about this past week that has prepared me for this!"). The building burned down just months before our visit, and the site is now marked with pricey lots and real estate signs.

Our last day at Camp always dawns too quickly and much too brightly after a night of pool playing and libation appreciation at the lodge. With handshakes and hugs, we left the Northwoods behind us as Sam and I drove farther north, directly into the Watton detox program commonly known as "haymaking."

Quoting LeGear many times over as I sweated pure Hamms on the hayfield, I clung to the dream that sustains me throughout the year: only 365 days until Fish Camp!

Fresh Spin on Fish Camping

I was trolling for a new lure last week when a sign in a shop window hooked me good: "We sell fidget spinners!"

It was Fish Camp time in Mercer, WI, and the world was my freshwater clam. Feeling flush because The Boys had forgotten to add more Hamms to my grocery list, I bit, swinging open the bait shop door that was rigged with a little bell that tinkled a merry, "Got one!"

Now, every kid in Baraga County—and every teacher who has been confiscating their fidget spinners this past year—can tell you a fidget spinner isn't made for fishing. It's a small hand-held toy with a ball bearing in the middle that kids spin between their fingers, all day long.

The difference between fidget spinners and other popular fads is that miracle called "marketing," which credits them with a therapeutic spin. Fidget spinners supposedly relieve stress and help hyperactive children focus. As a bonus, to the kids at least, they drive adults crazy.

And I already knew that, but I was kind of hoping someone had found a way to rig a treble hook onto one of the stupid gadgets. It would drive adult fish wild, causing them to strike like a junior high teacher at the end of a long day of confiscating fidget spinners.

Instead, I found the store owner and two boys who had set up shop inside his former domain. The kids happily demonstrated their fidget spinners. The man escaped outside for a therapeutic smoke. When he returned, I bought a Mepps spinner instead, then beat it for the Wampum Shop to check out the postcard selection.

Mepps spinners also relieve stress. They get me out of the cabin and into the sunshine on the Turtle Flambeau Flowage, where I drag them around weed beds and occasionally into trees in an effort to fool fish into biting.

Their shiny blades sparkle in the sunshine. Their bright bucktails cruise through the rippling water. Sometimes they disappear altogether, inhaled by another crazy pike. That's a little stressful, but in the very best of ways.

Back at the cabin, and with a good afternoon chop on the Flowage, I clipped my new spinner onto my line and headed out to fish with my husband. We worked shorelines and structure, weed beds and lily pads, putting the prod on passing pike with my gleaming new spinner and his old, chipped one.

We focused! They hit! Then the trip took a dark turn when a small pike I was unhooking shook himself free of my razor-sharp lure, burying one of the treble hooks deep into my right hand.

I was so shocked I forgot to cuss. I gave the hook a couple of tentative tugs, but it wouldn't budge. My husband rubbed his face, grimaced and said, "You're gonna' have to pull that out. And it's gonna' hurt like h--- when you do."

Both hands shook as I reached for my surgical instrument, which was the needle nose pliers rolling around in the bottom of the boat, and I gingerly gripped the shaft of the hook. A long minute passed as I sat, frozen in my seat, then my husband gulped uneasily and suggested, "Maybe there's a clinic in town . . ."

That was all I needed to hear. Lose an afternoon of fishing sitting in a clinic? I shut my eyes and ripped.

The Boys would have been more impressed if I'd brought back more Hamms. Apparently, you have to have exposed ligaments or, even better, bones dangling out of you if you want any pity at Fish Camp. All I had was a little bloody hole in my hand.

And memories of course, of a great week at Fish Camp with warm days on the Flowage, three-alarm fires on the grill at night and sunsets straight from heaven. In between we hooked one farsighted walleye, two bass with poor judgement, dozens of indiscriminating pike and eight juvenile muskies.

The Boys, my brother and buddies he grew up with on Chicago's South Side, were boys and the girls behaved just slightly better. Nobody was thrown out of a bar. Nobody fell out of a boat. If there was any swinging over late night politics, nobody connected.

I credit our stress-relieving spinners.

6. AT OUR SERVICE

Dad has Shuttle Seniority

In the wake of astronaut John Glenn's safe return from his Discovery shuttle mission, I would like to propose an even greater enterprise to all our good friends at NASA: let's send my dad into space!

First of all, I should probably point out that my dad has never expressed any interest whatsoever in space travel. Second, I would like to implore Mom to hide this paper RIGHT NOW! He'll grouse a little, but the look of surprise on his face when the NASA van comes for him will make it all worthwhile.

There are numerous reasons why I feel Bob Emerson should be the star of Senior Shuttle II. First of all, he is 78 years old, which gives him seniority over that young pup, John Glenn. Like Glenn, Dad also enjoyed an illustrious military career, during which he survived both the Battle of the Bulge and the Liberation of Paris.

I could linger on the Army stories, but then I'd lose this story's family rating. Besides, it is the differences between Dad and Glenn, not the common grounds they share, that prove only one man, "Mr. E," deserves the senior discount on the next shuttle out.

Glenn was sent into space to determine how we aging Americans might someday deal with the physical stresses of space travel. He prepared himself for this mission by achieving a remarkable level of fitness, which included a major weight loss, even though everyone knows when you're in space you're weightless, so what's the point in that?

Dad, our true representative of the people, would prepare for his trip into space the same way he prepares for his visits to Watton. First, he would question Mom to the point of distraction about what he should pack. Then he would leave most of it at home anyway, and blame Mom for what he was missing.

Dad has never been a slave to his body, and he would not start at age 78, even for the sake of his fellow 78-year-old Americans, many of whom look a lot like Dad. He's happy to take a walk to the coffee pot and back. If he could get a younger astronaut on the shuttle to fill his cup for him, he'd be even happier.

Of course, Senior Shuttle II riders can't just sit back, drink coffee and tell the youngsters about liberating Paris. Like Glenn, Dad would have to take an assortment of pills for the sake of scientific studies. And that is the one category where the former astronaut would be left, figuratively speaking, "eating Dad's space dust."

Unlike some older Americans who rail against pharmaceutical dependency, Dad takes his pills on a regular, downright religious basis. He can chew an aspirin like a breath mint, just in case there's a headache on the horizon, and has even been spotted eyeballing the grandkids' amoxicillin. You could count on Dad to take his pills in space, too—as long as Mom reminded him to pack them.

You could also count on Dad to bring back answers to the tough questions we future senior citizens have about space travel. Sure, we care about bone density and muscle loss and all that other scientific stuff too, but what about the issues that really hit close to home, such as:

1. What kind of TV reception can we expect to get in space?

2. How can you keep your quarters from floating out of your cup when you're winning at the slots?

3. How high can you crank up the shuttle thermostat before meltdown occurs?

The answers to all of the above are still up there in space, just waiting for Dad to bring them back to earth. As they say in the space program, "One small step for Bob, one giant leap for mankind!"

In a Military State

We are living in a military state.

A pair of Army boots stands at attention in our son's bedroom. His shaving supplies are neatly stowed in a kit beside the bathroom sink. Outside, a new red snowboard leans rakishly against the deck rail.

We are under siege. As Sam would say, "It's all good."

Sam has been in a military state since his tenth summer, when he visited an Army recruiting tent at the U.P. State Fair in Escanaba. He

Promoted to the rank of Dad, Sam is raising the kids right under the red, white and blue—but he still acts up

wanted the free dog tags, and the soldier on duty misspelled his name: Sam Bessonen.

He would wear them almost every day for the next eight years, until they slipped off during a cannonball into Wisconsin's Turtle Flambeau Flowage. The U.S. Government issued him another set that fall. This time, they got the name right.

This was not the future we would have charted for our middle child and only son. Sure, we let him go into the recruiting tent that day. We also let him fill his pockets with free taffy from the Sayklly's Candies booth, and tank up on free water from a religious group.

Why couldn't the kid have pursued a future in the church, or chocolates?

But that was not the stuff Sam was made of (though his Army dental records may indicate otherwise). Consequently, he returned home last Thursday night for a two-week leave after having served a full year in South Korea.

I hugged him hard when he got off the plane. It felt like he was made of bricks.

He's an inch and a half taller and several decibels louder than we remembered. He says you have to holler in the military, or you get in trouble. He chases me out of the dishpan, belly bumps his dad for the rank of alpha male, and talks long into the night with his two sisters, no telling allowed.

The phone rings for him daily, and friends we haven't seen in a while are filing in again. We cook too much, then wind up eating it on the run. Family closes in. After they leave, he makes time to visit them on their home turf as well.

He drives whatever vehicle is available, unless it is my mint green "chick mobile." Sam drove his dad's truck to his grandmother's house the other night, and the next day, we noticed some fresh skid marks on the road. I guess Sam was anxious to see his grandma.

He says he needs a haircut, because the hair on the sides of his head is actually showing. He picks dog and cat fur off his clothes before he goes out. Lacking adequate drawer space due to sibling displacement, he has a few clothes scattered around his bedroom.

Thank the Lord.

Even though he has been on his own for the past year and a half, he is constantly reminded to be careful. He snowboarded many times in Korea. He has a couple trips planned while home in the U.P. I will be sweating heavy artillery until he arrives home from them, safe and sound.

There's a lot left to do in the next nine days. We have more relatives and friends to see, wood to haul, fish to pursue and business to attend to. I still have to make him an apple pie, and brownies baked just the way he likes them: from a mix, with a handful of chocolate chips thrown in for Mom's special touch.

We need to cross country ski more, and watch a funny video together. Nobody laughs at comedies as loudly as Sam. He should play cards with his sisters, and tell his dad stuff he won't tell me. Nobody spills a secret as easily as my husband.

When Sam leaves home next week, he'll head for Fort Sill, OK. As far as Army bases go, it isn't prime realty, but he's happy to be stateside again. There he can hunt and fish and return home this summer, for another dip in the Flowage, and a belly bumping rematch with his dad.

I can't say where he'll go from there. I don't know what tomorrow has in store for him. But for now, Sam is sleeping, safe and sound on the couch, with the dog and cat illegally tucked against his feet.

It's all good.

Living the Dream

My middle brother, Mark, always knew what he wanted in life.

He wanted to go to the U.S. Military Academy at West Point. He'd have a career in the Army and pull rank on our dad, who gained and lost his stripes so often in WWII he may have inspired the invention of Velcro.

Mark worked for it. He studied hard, became a Boy Scout, and earned scouting's highest rank, Eagle. As a high school senior he cleared the final hurdle, a congressional nomination, and proudly applied for admission to West Point.

Then he got shot down.

The reason given was poor eyesight (Mark later realized it was his grades, and the system was just being kind). A pall fell over our family, because what had always mattered most to Mark had suddenly been taken away.

So, he went in the back door instead. He enrolled at a local college, joined ROTC, earned his degree and was proudly commissioned a 2nd Lieutenant in the U.S. Army. Twenty years later, Mark retired from the Army as a major.

The uniform still fit, and his attitude wasn't about to change, so one short year later Mark hired on as the Senior ROTC Instructor at Marmion Academy in Marmion, IL. Last week, I finally got to see my big brother in action.

Marmion is an all-male, Catholic-Benedictine college prep high school. Its ROTC program is elective, but about 80 percent of its students elect to participate. Mark says the students are more conservative than the teachers, all except for him.

We came to watch the Change of Command, an annual ceremony in which graduating battalion and company commanders hand over their duties to next year's leaders. There are precision drills, flashing sabers, marching music and snappy salutes, all by a small army of young men in uniform.

And right in the middle of it all was my brother, Mark.

Mark gave a short speech that he takes pride in making shorter every year, thanking the families in attendance and congratulating the graduates. He ended it with a gruff, "And rule number one will continue to apply." No explanation was given.

Then he walked down the line of seniors to shake their hands, only it was more like running the gauntlet, because Major Mark took some hits along the way from young men who had grown to know my brother way too well.

One senior tugged at Mark's uniform shirt. He was checking to make sure Mark had made good on his promise to wear the Christmas gift he'd given him, a political tee shirt that was strictly out of uniform. We could see the flash of red from halfway up the bleacher.

Another caught him up in a bear hug, and lifted him right off his feet. When he hit the ground again, Mark, still laughing, shook a warning finger at an even bigger senior down the line, and continued on.

"He was going to go all 'Dirty Dancing' on me, and lift me over his head," Mark later explained. "I told the kids beforehand, 'You do NOT hurt the Major!'"

When Mark emptied his uniform pockets that night, he found a bunch of spare change and a cigar, compliments of his ROTC graduates. He said last year he'd scored a lollipop, too.

Mark doesn't have a teaching degree: "I've got a Ranger tab—that matches your PhD." He instructs seniors only, arming them with leadership and life skills, including a solid grasp of the fourth amendment. It prohibits unreasonable search and seizure, and Mark believes young men are natural targets.

They have to memorize it, and they have to understand it. Mark knows it, too, because when I asked him to recite it over his morning coffee, he didn't miss a beat. I also got my answer to the question of rule number one: "What happens in my classroom, stays in my classroom."

Any subject is fair game for discussion in Major Mark's classroom. He says there has to be a safe place for kids to speak freely about anything, and at Marmion, it's senior ROTC.

He's been to West Point four times since he got shot down, invited by his former students to pin their 2nd Lieutenant bars onto their uniforms at their graduations. It's an honor Major Mark does not take lightly, and his wife, Joan, loves to be by his side when he's doing it.

Dream big, and don't be afraid to go in the back door.

Bringing Home World War II

My three older brothers and I grew up hearing war stories. Set in Europe during WWII, they featured characters with names like Baldy, Tom Dooley and our own Great Uncle Harry. Our very favorite stories, though, were the ones that starred our dad.

Dad lost his stripes almost as fast as he earned them. He once had to clean a hotel lobby with his toothbrush. Never mind that he landed with the seventh wave on Normandy Beach, and fought the Battle of the Bulge. All we knew was that stuff paled in comparison to our dad's Army antics.

Dad kept an old cardboard box stored in our apartment's hallway closet. If the four of us kids pestered him long enough, he would drag it out for inspection. Under its dusty lid lay WWII photos, goggles from a downed German pilot, dog tags, and other memorabilia from Dad's long march across Europe. We never experienced war, but we knew exactly how it smelled: like yellowed newspaper clippings, rusted metal and musty wool.

Our dad enlisted right after Pearl Harbor, and on his first day of basic training he slept through reveille. It was broad daylight when his drill sergeant finally nudged him awake, then sweetly asked him what he'd like for breakfast.

"Poached eggs and toast," Dad happily replied.

Oh, how Private Emerson paid for that breakfast!

The train that carried Dad away from basic training clattered right past his parents' home, on Vanderpoel Avenue on Chicago's South Side. He eventually hooked up with an outfit out of New York that was over 300 men strong. While shipping out, he befriended a New York City mounted policeman named Tom Dooley.

Dooley's and Dad's landing craft opened up into deep water at Normandy, and both men were drenched and terrified by the time they hit the sand. Dodging shells, they reached a wooded area where Dooley stripped off his uniform, then hung it over a branch to dry.

"Tom Dooley is wet," he announced. "The war can wait."

Dad didn't tell the whole story about Dooley until we kids were much older. One night, Dad and Dooley planned to head into a small town near France to hunt up some fun. Dad was winning at cards, so Dooley went on without him. The next day Dad was ordered to clean out a Jeep in which a fellow soldier had been shot and killed.

For Tom Dooley, the war was over.

Dad shared many stories over the years, but our very favorite happened in Paris, in 1944. He and a buddy were on R&R, Dad said, and were pretty well in their cups. They were standing alongside a group of officers, waiting to cross the Champs Elysse, when Dad, slightly bleary-eyed, thought he spotted a familiar face.

"Hey, buddy," Dad said to the officer in the middle. "You look familiar. Are you in our outfit?"

The officers on either side of the older man came to attention, glared at Dad, and looked to their superior. Then the senior officer smiled wide and put everyone at ease.

"I believe I am," the man told Dad. "They call me Ike."

Dad was at a port in Versailles, waiting to ship out to the Pacific, when V-J Day was proclaimed, and the war was over. He swore that when he was through with the service, he would never again pick up a gun. It was a promise he kept for the rest of his life.

Of the 300-plus men in his battalion who went to war, Dad was one of only 13 who lived to tell about it. In his children's eyes at least, he did a fine job indeed. Thank you for your service, Dad, and your stories.

7. PURSUIT OF FRUIT

Pails in Comparison

We had been in the berry patch for the better part of August, and the bottom of my bucket was finally covered. One of my raspberries was a bit off-color, though, and when I reached in to pluck it out, eight spindly legs clasped tightly onto my finger. I perished on the spot.

No, I didn't! I didn't even spill my berries, which is only allowed in case of bear attack, and even then, you had better have put up a good fight: "What, she only had one cub? You've still got two fingers! Now get out there and pick with 'em."

The spider lived, too, after a direct flight to freedom. In years to come he would balance hundreds of grandchildren on his eight knees, captivating them with the tale of the wild rodeo ride that ended when he got thrown by the legendary "Berry Picker."

Some folks use the term "berry picker" in a derisive manner, usually to describe lower Michiganders. But in a land where wealth is measured by the height of your woodpile or the heft of your netful of smelt, a berry picker with a full bucket is rich beyond compare.

Our children cut their teeth out in the berry patch, probably because they got a little gravel with their berries. Collectively, they equal or better my take, and that's with time out for toad chasing and aimless wandering. They're homegrown, after all, and thrive on free ranging.

My forefathers surely must have tramped the wilderness, too, and learned to live off the land. But where my husband's kin turned north, mine wandered south, tossing their berry buckets into the ditch at the first bus stop they encountered and happily hopping the express into the city.

I can recall exactly three harvests of natural produce from my youth on Chicago's South Side. The first was rhubarb that grew in a corner of my friend Cheri's yard. It was edible and free and we ate it the only way we knew how, which was raw.

"Thish ish shure good shtuff!" we would proclaim, our lips curling back from our teeth in your classic raw rhubarb grimace. Then we would spit it out and head to the store for candy, just like my forefathers did while they were waiting for the bus.

The next harvest came later in the summer, when the Shebelskis' cherry tree ripened. Unfortunately, it was located behind the fence in their backyard, and Mr. and Mrs. Shebelski had wisely produced five little Shebelskis to guard it.

We neighborhood kids quickly learned that if you got John, Mike, Mary, Stevie or Susie really mad, they would pelt us with the goods. The harvest would literally be upon us! Of course, the other 50 or so weeks of the year we all got along just fine.

The third and final picking came in the fall, when the prickly-coated chestnuts in Marquette Park deepened to a mahogany hue. They were bitter and inedible, even for kids who chewed raw rhubarb, but a line from "The Christmas Song" inspired us to give them a shot.

Kids are born arsonists, and the image of "chestnuts roasting on an open fire" sparked a real dandy. We decided to cook some up in the only place we knew that was shielded from both the wind and public view: right outside Henry Steinberg's basement apartment.

A picking crew was quickly dispatched to Marquette Park to fill their bike baskets with chestnuts, while the rest of us got busy collecting wood. Because it was the inner city, our fuel consisted of gum wrappers, discarded cigarette packs and a pile of dried leaves.

In the end, we ruined a lot of chestnuts and our relationship with Mrs. Steinberg, who quit making her delicious apple pancakes for Henry and his little friends after we succeeded in smoking her out of their apartment.

And what did we learn from the experience? Don't believe everything you sing!

Berry picking in the U.P. isn't any easier, but it's infinitely more rewarding. The bounty is there for the taking. All you have to do is make peace with the fact it takes a while and involves a little blood loss. Summers are short in the U.P., but berries guarantee they'll be sweet.

Wild strawberries are first up, in mid-June or early July. They're the size of a pea, and keep you busy picking until the big, juicy domestics ripen, primarily in Chassell. You pick those, too, but you have to pay the farmer before he'll let you and your strawberries leave his field.

Blueberries and raspberries ripen next. Blueberries grow low to the ground on buggy, sandy plains. Raspberries grow in clear cuts, also with bugs included. Bears also favor both fruits, but typically shy away from pickers, especially ones who are loudly shrieking, "SPIDER!!!!"

Blackberries end the picking season on an up note: it's you, shrieking again, this time from contact with their thick, thorn-studded poles and branches. You won't find any "pick your own" signs posted outside blackberry patches. Growers can't afford the liability.

The harvest season ends with the arrival of fall and the school bus, which ferries our picking crew out of the patch to freedom. A freezer full of fruits, jams and pie fillings will see us nicely through the next three seasons, a fine reward for time well bent.

But it would have been a whole lot easier if the Shebelski kids had been guarding the berries.

Berry Picker Blues

I was hunkered down in the heat, bent over my work, when the sound of a car approaching shot fear through my heart.

Where was the child?!

Just a few feet away from me, a tiny "Finding Dory" cap suddenly popped up just above the brush line. Uncharacteristically silent (the child can chat up a clothes pole), she watched the car pass by, then sank down again to play in the sand.

I smiled as I dropped a handful of blueberries into my pail. Our granddaughter is learning the way of our world. It's called "stealth mode" during berry picking season.

It's stealth mode during a lot of seasons around here, owing to the fact we live in the sticks. We don't have Sam's Club, Costco or even a Meijer's, unless we're Marquette shoppers. We shop natural resources instead.

The thing about shopping natural resources is, we naturally want to keep them to ourselves. Unlike store aisles that are clearly labeled, the U.P. doesn't point shoppers toward its produce sections--or its meat or fish ones, either.

Natural resource shoppers are always on the hunt or on the pick, and they learn to scout out their terrain. Raspberries and blackberries both grow in areas that have been recently logged. Blueberries, like the rain in Spain, are mainly on the Plains.

Berries, berries everywhere, but the promise of pie sweetens the deal for picker/packer Gwen

So are we these days, for the past couple of weeks at least, ever since the night my husband asked me out for an evening cruise on the Baraga Plains. I brushed my hair, scrubbed the garden dirt off my hands and applied a fresh coat of bug repellent. A girl never knows when she's going to get lucky!

And we did, because our scouting trip led us to the promised land. It promised many days, afternoons and a couple of very buggy evenings of creeping, stooping and sometimes sitting beside low-lying blueberry bushes, plucking free fruit.

I've had a case of the blues ever since.

My fingers are slightly curled, stuck in the "pluck" position. I have bug bites where bad girls get tattoos, and the knees and backside of my comfiest work jeans are sporting the berry picker's badge of honor: lots of telltale blue spots.

We usually pick in the mornings, because the bugs tend to sleep in. There are other berry pickers too at times, usually a fair distance away, and we respect each other's space. We don't wave. They don't either. We're there to pick. It's the way of the sticks.

Most of all, we don't talk. If someone asks if we've been picking blueberries, we say yes, because it's hard to lie when you have leaves in your hair and blue spots on your butt. When they ask where we've been picking, we say "The Plains." Then we say "Good-bye."

We are not rude. We are berry pickers, and the season is short but sweet. There are cups and pails and sometimes even hubcaps to fill while out in the field, and freezer bags and canning jars to fill back at home. Then we can go fishing again, which we do "In the water," and hunting, which we do "In the woods."

Enjoy all of our natural resources, unless we get there before you, and please watch out for our grandchildren. Good-bye.

How We Like Them Apples

Question: If an apple falls from a tree in the woods, do I have to can it?

Answer: Absolutely not! I can also bake it, sauce it, press it or eat it outright, taking care not to drop any seeds that may result in yet another dang apple tree in the future.

Johnny Appleseed had his way with the U.P., which is once again flush with apples this fall. Not every tree is producing, but the ones bearing fruit are looking a little Ozzy (as in the scary trees in The Wizard of Oz, not the even scarier rock star), and acting it, too.

We are literally pummeled by apples. They clunk me on the head when I mow under the apple trees. Then they get caught in the mower blades, spraying applesauce all over the lawn. That in turn spreads even more seeds, which will grow more apples to clunk me on the head in the future.

I can deal with clunks on the head. I just wear a hard hat when I mow. It is the sheer abundance of fruit that's getting me down this season, because our family's coat of arms is the universal symbol for recyclables. In other words, we do not waste.

We don't take disposal lightly. Much of what we try to cast off gets caught on our rock fence for future consideration. We eat what we grow, if we can beat the deer to it. If God should put free fruit before us, we go all Adam and Eve over it.

And if Facebook is any indicator, we are not alone in our inability to say no to Mother Nature.

Every day finds another half dozen posts of gleaming canning jars neatly lined up on countertops, brimming with the bounty of the fall harvest. Produce is our drug of choice in the U.P., and Mason and Ball are our enablers.

I don't post, because I'd have to clean my kitchen first, but all the signs are there. We have pails full of apple peels out on the deck. We can't see out our windows because they're steamed up from the canner. When I go to the store, I automatically grab another handful of canning lids, just out of habit.

My hands are stained worse than a smoker's. My hair hangs limp from the humidity. I thought I was starting to see spots, but my eye doctor assures me it's just fruit flies. He sees a lot of that this time of year in the U.P.

The good news is, winter is right around the bend. It covers the last few apples in a blanket of white, grinding the apple processing machine to a halt. After a season of bounty, we're hoping the apple trees take a little rest next summer.

It would give us more time to pick and put up berries.

8. THINGS OF BEAUTY

Capris Here—Run for Cover!

Every once in a while, the wonderful world of fashion falls under the delusion that all women are created like Jackie Kennedy.

Elegant and lithe, Jackie set the standard for fashion in her day. When she donned a pillbox hat, women across America embraced the bell boy look. Jackie also favored simple, figure-flattering shifts. Suddenly, we were a nation of Jello molds.

She even looked good in jodhpurs, those horseback riding pants that feature skinny legs and big, built-in hips. Women everywhere get a little credit for letting that ball drop, but I am sorry to report that after over a half century of healing, the fashion world has resurrected another of Jackie's favorites: capri pants.

Capris are designed to be close-fitting to accentuate the female form, sporting a hidden zipper and tiny button or clasp, again with the form. What separates a capri from, say, trousers you might actually wear in public, is the fact they stop mid-range between your ankle and knee.

If you accessorize with a U.S. president, you might succeed in carrying off the look. If not, like the rest of us, you are looking at big trouble, starting with a capital "c."

All of the clothing stores, from major to minor to gently used, are sporting bulging racks of unfinished pants this season. Women who usually shop in the petite section now enjoy free range of the entire women's clothing department. For those who shop size regular, there is nowhere to run.

There are capri dress pants, capri sweat pants, capri jeans and I think I may have seen a capri bathing suit bottom. They come in slim fit and baggy, with pockets or without, in pull-on or zippered, as well as those button-fly that make timing so crucial when considering potty stops.

The style is based on the presumption that there is something strikingly beautiful about the female ankle. Paired with just the right shoes, capris are supposed to make you look young and carefree and ready to go sailing with one of those guys who wears deck shoes and no socks.

The reality is not pretty, especially in the spring-forsaken U.P. where March comes in like a lion, goes out like a lion, and the word "sailing" is usually preceded by "rummage." So, before you go out and buy some capris to match those pillbox hats and shifts, let's consider the consequences.

First of all, spring will not officially arrive in the U.P. until the rest of the world is in the full throes of summer. You can wear capri pants with your Sorel boots, but they won't keep the snow out, and you will spend both weeks of summer explaining why you have felt burns circling your calves.

When the snow finally leaves, the bugs wake up. If your capris have loose legs, they will act as a funnel for stinging insects, directing them to regions you ought not scratch in public. Or, they will simply feast on your nicely turned ankles, reducing them within minutes to nicely turned sausages.

If you still insist upon wearing capris, you'll have to get some cute little shoes to go with them. You cannot clomp around town in capri pants and your garden shoes and expect someone to ask you out on their yacht. Floppy Nikes with laces that drag in the dust have their place, and it isn't Hyannis Port.

You cannot wear bobby socks, slouch socks, knee socks or your kids' soccer socks with your capri pants. You can wear those little footie socks with the pompom in the back, the ones that cut off the circulation across the tops of your feet, but the pom poms have to match your pants or you'll be arrested by the fashion police. They're the ones sporting black capris.

Finally, if you expect to pay less just because the fashion industry stopped before your pants cuffs hit the tops of your shoes, think again! Elegance doesn't come cheap you know, and neither do capris, but they will prepare you for the next fashion resurrection on the horizon: Jodhpurs for Fall.

Oscars Out of Fashion

I feel awfully good about the way I'm dressed today.

I watched the Academy Awards last night, and noticed that on probably one of the most important evenings of their lives, most of the women chose to dress down and sometimes out.

Several just wore their nighties, I think, but more favored gowns with lavish bustles and long, flowing trains, resulting in an unfortunate deficit of material for finishing off their tops. They really could have afforded to hitch those gowns up a bit, I think, and lose that frightened look in their eyes.

An actress who once played a gravity-challenged nun and has been trying to get back down to earth since was tightly wrapped with a bow on top that barely secured the package. Another woman wore a shimmery shift made entirely out of gold American Express cards.

She should have left home without it.

She was picking up an Oscar for fashion design, of course. From the accompanying clip, it appeared that her movie was about men who dressed like women and liked to dance around in the desert. The men's dresses were pretty lame, too.

Men usually have it much easier. You can bet that Adam's leaf fit him like a charm. But even the men at the Oscars couldn't quite swing the pants/shirt/tie/jacket formula. One wore a collarless shirt with his tux for that, "I don't care, well yeah, I deeply do" look. Many skipped their ties altogether.

It's a bitter blow when the tie Dad did up for you before you left home finally comes unknotted. But there's times when a guy just has to swallow his pride, turn to the old man seated beside him on the bus ride to the Oscars, and ask, "Do you do Windsors?"

A lot of men wore black shirts with their tuxedos, which went a long way toward concealing the fact they forgot their ties, too. You can't beat black for hiding a stain or an oversight. At least none of the men wore ugly dresses like those guys dancing in the desert.

Now, you may be wondering, "Who does Nancy think she is, commenting on other people's wardrobes?" especially if you've seen me around town. Well, I am somebody who watched the Oscars wearing baggy blue jogging pants and a floral turtleneck while scribbling vicious notes on a scratch pad.

And really, isn't that what being a fashion critic is all about?

The real reason I tuned in to the awards was not so much to criticize, though it was a lovely bonus, but to be able to write in a knowing and animated manner about this year's best movies. When you live 40 miles from the nearest movie theater, and motor oil isn't on sale at Shopko, it's hard to warrant a road trip to a movie that will be available at the co-op just two short years from now.

We did get out to see The Lion King twice and Forrest Gump once, but after you get past the warthog with gas jokes and the "Didn't those scenes with Gump in historical situations look REAL?" comments, there's not a whole lot left to say.

So, based on cultural tidbits I picked up Monday at the Oscars, I can now communicate on a much higher level:

- What was with that goofy dance Travolta did in "Pulp Fiction?"

- Why do foreign films all look like bad movies from the '60's?

- Did you catch that lady wearing the credit cards?

I for one won't be taking my fashion cues from the movie stars at the Oscars. On the most important night of my life, I wore a wedding gown from J.C. Penney with a high neck and no train because I didn't want people dancing on my new white dress all night.

And what am I wearing today? Well, there's my CPR instruction card, library card, insurance card, thrift store punch card...

Mr. Rogers Rocked It

Remember how Mr. Rogers used to come home from wherever he was, pull on his cardigan, tie on his sneakers and begin another Beautiful Day in the Neighborhood? No? Oh, go watch sports already!

If you are still with me, you are even sportier than you think, because for the first time in his soft-spoken life, Mr. Rogers was wildly ahead of the times. He wasn't dressing down for children. He was totally rocking Athleisure Wear.

(Today, the cardigan would be your favorite team's jersey, but Mr. Rogers liked everybody equally).

In a society that celebrates sloth, celebrities who are already making too much money are making even more by hawking athletic clothing for people who have no intention of breaking a sweat. From sneakers to headbands, with a lot of disturbing Spandex in between, Athleisure Wear is upscale clothing that can be worn at the gym or on the street.

Nancy and her BFF, Sue, rock the Athleisure Wear look at Vermillac Lake in Covington

Ideally, you'd look equally out of place at either location. In today's radical fashion world, you will fit right in, in high style.

We were not always a nation of athleisure wearers, as evidenced by our own hometown newspaper's weekly history page. In a reprinted front-page photo from a 1950s ballgame at a local field, the fans looked like they had all come straight from a wedding, possibly their own.

The men seated in the bleachers wore dress pants and white shirts. The women all wore dresses and shoes with heels. The only people wearing baseball caps and jerseys were the actual players, and all their bills were facing in the right direction.

I will withhold comment on what fans wear nowadays. Instead, I will comment freely on what I wear, because that will not generate scathing Letters to the Editor. I sit right across from him in the office, and can tell Barry what I think in person. And I'm not very well dressed when I do it.

Barry wisely tuned me out long ago, but when I come home from wherever I was before that, I pull on a tee shirt and jogging pants. Oftentimes, I am already wearing them. The tee shirt is from my favorite French designer, St. Vincent DePaul. The pants are from the clearance rack at Target, or "tar-JEAY."

The backside of my jogging pants is all shiny from my dedication to reading magazines. The knees are snagged from berry picking. The white racing stripes on the legs indicate whether I am vertical or horizontal.

My tee shirts sport logos ranging from Fishigan State University to the patron saint of teenagers, Aeropostale. I don't care whose shirt I'm wearing, so long as it doesn't bind while I'm reading or berry picking. It also shouldn't clash with my shiny joggers.

Country singer Carrie Underwood, R&B artist Rihanna and actress Kate Hudson are all selling the Athleisure Wear look this season, but I'm not biting. It's overpriced, frequently revealing, and lacks indicator stripes on the legs. And in just a few short years, I can buy it all on the cheap from Vinny's.

Until then, I'll keep it loose and slightly shiny so we can all continue to enjoy a Beautiful Day in the Neighborhood.

"Alien Stompers" All the Rage

Reebok has released a new shoe designed to stomp aliens. They're called "Alien Stompers."

Before you start scrambling to find your green card, I should clarify that the aliens of interest are the kind from outer space. We don't stomp aliens in America! We just threaten them with our political candidates.

As if that isn't news enough in the wonderful world of footwear, it gets even better. Consumers are hoppin' mad and raising a stink on anti-social media because Reebok didn't make enough Alien Stompers for the rompin' stompin' market.

I would like to take this opportunity to lay the blame on Sigourney Weaver.

Sigourney starred in four installments of the popular Alien movie franchise. The first was titled "Alien." The second was "Aliens." The third was called "Even More Aliens" and the fourth, "Everybody Loves Aliens."

That is called "taking poetic license," a valuable tool we journalists use to dodge boring fact-finding and costly litigation. Because she majored in acting instead of journalism, Sigourney made scads of money. But she also had to do it all in the popular series, including filling some pretty big shoes in outer space.

Sigourney's character in the Alien movies is an extremely fit, perpetually sweaty soldier who just wants to make the world safe from aliens. The aliens she constantly battles are slimy, irritable, and have bad teeth. Worst of all, they're screamers.

She survives bursts of gunfire, oceans of slime and a very disturbing birth scene (spoiler alert: Daddy wasn't from here) to save the world from even more alien movies. She fails miserably, but we Americans love our sequels almost as much as our footwear.

And Hollywood listens, because in the second movie, made possible by all those surviving aliens, Sigourney rocks some new sneakers. They're big and red and white and high rise of course because alien stomping can get very messy.

As a discerning movie goer and footwear fan, I would question the Velcro closures. Velcro clogs with lint. Can you imagine trying to fasten up in the morning after a long night of alien stomping? Otherwise, I am good with the concept.

However, the same does not hold for my fellow earthlings.

On Alien Day, which is April 26th, Reebok celebrated both corporate greed and the Alien franchise by re-releasing Sigourney's shoes, this time on a nationwide scale. Besides cutting us seriously short, Reebok made them in men's sizes only, and its checkout system checked out.

The crowds went wild, as exhibited by frustrated consumer A. Carboni's desperate tweet: "oh lord help me they are in my cart BUT I CAN'T CHECK OUT WHYYY???

We don't know, A. Carboni. Could be sunspots. Could be aliens in Human Resources. Maybe you just need to rethink your footwear, since the originals went for $175 or, shortly after noon last Tuesday, $800 on eBay.

A Reebok spokesman calmly explained that men's sizes 3-12 are typically unisex. He was never heard from again. The checkout glitch was also resolved by Reebok shortly after noon on Alien Day, which just leaves us wanting more.

Stay tuned for the next regularly scheduled Alien Day, when Nike counters with Everybody Loves Aliens Flip Flops (they shed the slime!) in men's, women's, children's, orthopedic and, of course, alien's sizes.

9. MUSIC TO MY EARS

Campbell Strikes a Chord

A few weeks back, we went to see an old guy sing Glen Campbell songs. The cool thing was, the old guy was Glen Campbell.

If the kid behind the counter is giving you your coffee at the senior rate, even though it's clearly premature, you know Campbell as a country/pop singer. He's entertained for over a half century with songs like "Wichita Lineman," "Rhinestone Cowboy" and so many more.

As a kid, I listened to him on our kitchen radio that served up the morning news with our corn flakes. It was followed by a steady stream of mostly easy listening that set the beat for easy living as a child of the 1960s and '70s.

Nowadays I enjoy Campbell's music at Fish Camp, an annual gathering of former Chicago South Side delinquents at a lake in Mercer, WI. Spin master Bob LeGear stacks his deck of CDs with Campbell hits to help soothe the savage beasts, present company included.

We came, we went, and as usual the fish barely noticed. But shortly after returning home from Fish Camp in early June, I fixed my bleary eyes on the summer concert schedule for the Big Top Chautauqua in Bayfield, WI, and swallowed the hook.

The Big Top Chautauqua is an organization that hosts class music acts all summer long, in a 900-seat canvas tent set up at the base of a ski hill. Joan Baez, The Temptations and The Beach Boys have taken to its stage. At the end of June, it would welcome Glen Campbell.

I could have dropped my tackle box, but my husband makes me leave the sorry outfit at the door. We checked our schedules--open!-- our finances--adequate! --then secured two cheap seats for "Glen Campbell, the Farewell Tour."

Farewell tours are not uncommon among entertainers. Some schedule them on a fairly regular basis. But for Glen Campbell, there

Jammin' buddies Laura & Emily (they play Campbell, too) pose between chords

would be no coming back. Last fall, at age 76, he was diagnosed with Alzheimer's.

The disease that robs people first of their memories and then their lives is becoming as mainstream as cancer. Nearly everyone is affected by it in some way, either through a loved one's struggles or their own. My mother-in-law has Alzheimer's. In our love for her, we suffer from it as well.

Campbell had already had the disease for a few years. Its effects vary, and his ability to string together sentences is diminished, but take it from the cheap seats: Campbell is still king.

The Big Top was filled to its billowing capacity by a crowd that spilled out onto the grassy fields surrounding the tent. After the house band warmed up the audience, Campbell walked onto the darkened stage. When the spotlight found him, the applause was an explosion.

He was wearing jeans and a shiny blue cowboy shirt that looked just right on Campbell. The youthful band behind him, including three of his children, was dressed mostly in black that looked just right on the kids. After a friendly wave and a "Howdy!", he dove into song.

You usually have to wait awhile to hear an entertainer's most recent hit or signature song. With so long a trail of hits in his wake, Campbell's deck was stacked as good as LeGear's, with "Gentle on my Mind," "By the Time I Get to Phoenix" and many, many more.

The songs sounded a bit craggier, the inflections a little different, but it was classic Campbell. Hit after hit flowed out into the tent and the night, with the audience occasionally rising to its feet, then settling down again because really, most of us were around when he first sang them.

Many performers say a few words between songs, probably just to catch their breath. Alzheimer's makes it tough to communicate, but with his beaming grin and genuine love of entertaining, Campbell did just fine, delivering short, poignant comments throughout the night.

He thanked us all for coming, thanked the people who wrote the songs, and thanked his kids for playing with him: sons Cal on drums and Shannon on guitar, and his daughter, Ashley, on keyboard and banjo. All three were in their mid- to late-20s.

And it was great to see the kids working with and watching out for their dad. Campbell had prompters onstage to help him remember the music and lyrics. When he forgot to look, Ashley would smile over at him and whisper, "It's in G (chord), Dad," or tell him the first few words of a song.

She cued him about three times on one song, and when he finally noticed, he grinned at her and grumbled, "I know—I'm doin' it my way!" The audience loved it, bursting into applause for them both.

And he loved us back, playing to the whole house as he strode back and forth across the stage. Sometimes he'd point his mike our way, feeding us a few lines we already knew by heart, and was genuinely touched by our enthusiastic, if not terribly melodic, response.

I never knew how great a guitarist he was—it's hard to tell over the radio—until that night in the Big Top, when words often failed him but his playing was spot-on. He and Ashley joined in playing a duet that made you wonder how a guy who's 76 can move so fast, and why he has to be saying good-bye.

Then all too soon, Campbell started to wilt under the lights, first tugging at the collar of his shirt, then asking the audience if it wasn't getting hotter in the tent. At the end of the next song, he abruptly spun around and walked to the back of the stage.

His kids exchanged nervous glances, then together they ushered him back for one last hit. When Campbell finished, the band stepped forward together, arms linked around one another, as he made his parting comment: "I love playing with my kids."

The audience rose to its feet in a thunderous ovation as the group left the stage. We kept on clapping, but Campbell made good on his farewell. Finally, reluctantly, so did we.

We Want Another Rock?

An initiative is currently underway to bring another rock to Upper Michigan.

If you farm, garden or slide into bases in the U.P., you are well aware that we've already got lots of rocks, exceeded only by our weeds. Our annual snowfall, measured in feet rather than inches, actually comes in a distant third.

Our forefarmers stacked rocks to create rock fences, thereby assuring they would always have a place to park their broken farming equipment. Our foremothers brewed weeds into dandelion wine to get themselves through yet another haymaking season.

That is a purely subjective observation. I am the one who has a haymaking problem. I'd much rather have a dandelion wine problem, but our one and only batch tasted light and weedy, with undertones of something the kids had stepped in.

Wine making is a God-given right that most of us should give back. It consists of picking fruit, extracting the juice, fermenting and bottling and then giving it all away at Christmas, preferably in exchange for store-bought adult beverages.

Eventually your friends, like the USPS, refuse to accept hazardous liquids. You resign yourself to drinking alone and arguing with yourself over the attributes of a 2009 chokecherry vs. a 2009 chokecherry, different bottle.

The argument for bringing yet another rock into the U.P. is totally unrelated, but you cannot expect smooth transitions from a seasoned (season of 2009) homemade wine drinker. This rock is a rock star. We want him to come up here and sing to us.

Kid Rock, or as his mom called him when he got into trouble, Robert James Ritchie, is the total package: singer, songwriter, record producer and actor. He has frequently sung about the U.P., but he has never actually sung in it.

A radio station in Marquette is currently petitioning to right this grievous wrong. Chip "the Fat Man" Arledge, host of radio station 100.3 The Point, is heading up the effort to roll Rock up north.

"He goes over to Mackinac Island, but he's never played a concert here," Arledge stated in an article somebody else wrote. "And this is like his signature song. I mean, this is a huge record, biggest selling record of 2008, but yet he never plays up here."

The song Arledge is referring to is "All Summer Long." Set in the U.P., it is a tribute to young love, questionable choices and scanty beachwear. It was released in 2008. Two years after, Rock shot his "Born Free" video at Pictured Rocks National Lakeshore.

Six short summers later, you can't book a room in Munising.

You can't entirely blame Kid Rock for the mania that is Pictured Rocks, with visitors up from 560,000 in 2015 to 723,000 the following year. The National Park Service celebrated its 100th birthday in 2016. They were probably thinking there would be cake.

And Arledge is thinking there will be a Rock concert in the U.P. someday soon, though maybe not in Munising, with ticket prices even Upper Michiganders can afford, if he can just secure 15,000 signatures politely asking Rock to visit.

Book your lodgings now! I'll bring the wine.

Disco Drops the Ball

Astronomers everywhere are watching the skies and tapping their toes to the Bee Gees as they wait for a giant disco ball to plummet to earth.

You read it here first, only because I read it somewhere else first and that is how the wacky news world works. It was on CNN, the official news source for people who are anti-FOX, and provides the following important message:

A giant disco ball is falling to earth, and just like the musical era that spawned it, we have nowhere to run!

According to the responsible journalist who actually researched the subject, the disco ball is a Reflective Satellite. It was launched by a private company called Rocket Lab, which also brought us the Pensive Satellite, the Contemplative Satellite and the Moody Teen Satellite.

Just kidding! No, the satellite named "The Humanity Star" does not come equipped with moods. Instead, it is made of carbon fiber, and has 65 reflective panels designed to bounce the sunlight back to earth, just like a giant disco ball.

The satellite was launched to encourage earthlings everywhere to never forget disco, lest we repeat the insanity. Also, "to think a little differently about our lives, actions, and what is important for humanity."

The Humanity Star, much like your popular modern-day stars, had "no specific function, except as a spectacle." As it spun across the night sky it would blink and flash, just like a Kardashian, causing us to contemplate our place in the cosmos.

Of course, not everybody is excited by the concept of a giant disco ball spinning through space. Classical music lovers might prefer a whirling candelabra. Country music fans would get a kick out of a rolling keg.

Astronomers would just prefer empty space. Terms like "space graffiti" and "space garbage" are being tweeted about by the folks who make their livelihood keeping a lookout overhead. They're already trying to see around several thousand satellites orbiting the earth. Bad art aloft is just one more bump in their road.

The satellite, also like your modern-day stars, had a projected shelf life of about nine months before it fizzled out. Unfortunately, something went horribly wrong, besides the fact we forgot to look up at it, because its attention span has failed and now it's falling back to earth.

That is the problem with the stuff we shoot up into space. It sometimes spits it back.

The cosmos may be vast, but it has standards too you know, and a ball inspired by an era of bad music clearly doesn't cut the mustard. Just one month into its near year-long assignment, space got fed up with all that blinking and flashing and gave The Humanity Star the boot.

While we all look up to the stars above, wondering which one might come down and fall on our heads, The Humanity Star is actively taking the leap, hopefully dissolving into the something-sphere before it rains down reflectively.

Be sure to watch the skies for Rocket Lab's next installation, the Moody Teen Satellite. It will be especially challenging to spot in its Goth phase as it slumps across the sky, kicking other satellites out of its way-- but it's still a big step up from the disco ball.

Footnote: Ironically, this story was being typed even as The Humanity Star was disintegrating last Thursday, scientifically proving old news really is good news--until I sit down to write again next week.

10. FUN WITH FADS

Barbie Gets Her Grooves On

Of all the earth-shattering things that happened in the news last week, like snow in our Nation's Capital and the presidential race in general, I'd guess the biggest is that Barbie is gaining weight.

(That's right. I have a terrible nose for news. It's the real reason I'm not shoveling in Washington right now or holding my ears in Iowa).

Apparently, a well-rounded Barbie is a very good thing, because it makes little girls feel good about their own bodies. Meanwhile, little boys everywhere will continue to pop Barbies' heads off, just because they can.

Like it or not, America learned a lot about Barbie this past week. Like, her full name is Barbara Millicent Roberts, and she first appeared on toy store shelves in 1959, and every second of every minute, a new Barbie goes flying off the shelf into another unsuspecting shopper's cart.

I'm pretty sure the purchases are intended, but you can't tell with Barbies. They're always changing, pursuing new hair colors and careers. Unlike G.I. Joe, whose craggy features remained the same throughout my evil brothers' boyhoods, Barbie gets a do-over almost daily.

In the beginning, she was blonde or brunette. Then she became black or Hispanic, which was a good thing. Then you cut her hair, which was a bad thing because it devalued your investment and caused Ken to lose interest, though nobody ever thought Ken was much of a catch, anyway.

Starting out as simply a party girl--she debuted in a zebra-striped leotard--Barbie has enjoyed over 180 careers in the course of just under 60 years, from an RN to an astronaut. She even ran for president in the 1990s. Nowadays, she might have had a shot.

But Barbie has a bigger agenda these days, and it's all about self-worth. The 11 ½ inch doll with a tiny waistline, legs up to here and a bust that could break your foot if you stepped on it in the dark is undergoing a radical transformation.

She is finally getting some meat on her bones, besides what she's already sporting above her waist.

Barbie is about to come out in three new body sizes: tall (wasn't she already?), petite and curvy. And in the words of Dr. Seuss' *The Cat in the Hat,* who is also kind of ample in the hips, "That is not all, oh no, that is not all!"

Barbie will be sold in 23 new, eye-popping designs this spring. She'll feature varying skin tones, hair colors and styles, outfits, and of course, body types. I saw them myself, on my very own computer, and I'd have to say it's kind of scary.

Little girls with curvy figures, stiletto heels, violet hair and disturbing bust lines will now have a doll they can look up to. Same goes for petite girls who have blue hair, tall girls with spiky hair, etc. On an up note, Barbie might finally be safe from little boys.

If you give it some careful thought, and I have given it way too much already, Barbie is not the first to fall to marketing's warped image of what we Americans need to see.

I give you Tony the Tiger, Smokey the Bear and the Campbell Kids. May they rest in peace.

Tony the Tiger is all about Sugar Frosted Flakes, and he used to look it. He was a fluffy, friendly tiger who visited kids at the breakfast table, encouraging them to eat more cereal caked with processed sugar by roaring into their tender ears, "THEY'RE GRRRRRRRREAT!"

Now Tony has gone all buff, with a waistline almost as tiny as Barbie's and an even bigger, albeit hairier, chest. Same goes for Smokey, who lumbers around the woods giving bear hugs to people who put out their campfires. Like that's not disturbing, either.

I worry for Smokey, who has also dropped some serious weight. In fact, I'm not entirely sure he'll make it through the winter, which will no doubt inspire a new line labeled, "Barbie the Smokey." She's really going to rock that ranger hat! Let's just hope she doesn't try to douse any campfires with her hairspray.

Finally, we had the Campbell Kids, those apple-cheeked, chubby little cartoon spokespersons for Campbell's soup. They were absolutely darling. They made you truly believe that Campbell's soup was "Mm, mm, good!" They just had a little weight problem.

Was it the cream of chicken or the cream of mushroom soup that did their careers in? Nobody knows for sure, but somewhere along the line the Kids vanished, replaced by real live slender children, and "Mm, mm, good!" hasn't been as good since.

From a purely subjective viewpoint, I would advise Barbie to tread lightly on her new path to social acceptance. In a fickle world run by people raised on Sugar Frosted Flakes, growing a curve could get a girl tossed out of the game.

It just might be time for Barbie to finally settle down with someone solid and dependable. I am thinking G.I. Joe.

Swedes Make a Clean Sweep

As your hometown newspaper's self-proclaimed editor of all things nobody else wants to write about, I give you: Swedish Death Cleaning!

First of all, a disclaimer: I have no intention of doing your Swedish Death Cleaning. I'm too busy typing. It's something you have to do for yourself, no matter what your lineage, if you want to be on the cutting edge of de-cluttering.

It all began three years ago when Marie Kondo, who is not Swedish but sure cleans like it, published her book, *the life-changing magic of tidying up*. We Americans scooped it up, along with a bunch of other stuff of course, in our never-ending quest to find our dining room tables.

We just love our stuff! And apparently the rest of the world does, too, because Kondo's books were selling like hotcakes, and for good reason. Instead of telling folks to just throw away things they don't want, she encourages them to only keep "what brings you joy."

Before you knew it, readers everywhere were getting their joy on by emptying out their houses. They pitched stuff by the truckloads, then neatly folded and stored what was left in their bedside night stands.

Kondo carved a rewarding career out of de-cluttering, literally cleaning up on cleaning up. There were lectures, TV appearances, follow-up books and videos on how to store what had survived the purge.

For thrift shoppers, it was the very best of times. And it's about to get even better.

It was only a matter of time before someone encouraged us to cut even deeper. That would be the 80-something-year-old Swedish artist Margareta Magnusson with her new book, *The Gentle Art of Swedish Death Cleaning*.

The Swedish term for it is "dostadning," with little dots over the vowels like the stuff we love to buy from IKEA. Magnusson's message, which will debut this January along with her book, is simple. Declutter before you check out so you don't burden your survivors with all your stuff.

If you don't think your stuff will burden your family, you are not my children. The girls could not contain their mirth when I strongly hinted at future grandchildren by reverently presenting them with my old maternity tops.

"They're all pleated and poofy!"

"I'd look like an upside-down cupcake!"

And our son is none too excited, either, about someday inheriting my rusty tackle box stuffed with dented spoons, bobbers that sink and bent spinners trailing threadbare bucktails.

"You really need to get rid of those."

Magnusson's pitch list is pretty much the same as Kondo's, including clothes you don't wear, dishes you don't eat off of, and any jewelry the kids made from macaroni. She does it all with "Scandinavian humor and wisdom," helping ease our pain when breaking up proves hard to do.

Ideally, you should begin your Swedish Death Cleaning when you are middle aged and still nimble enough to haul your own stuff to the curb, though I'm sure our kids would be happy to assist me. Along the way, Magnusson promises, your life will become both simpler and more worth living.

I might even be able to latch my tackle box again.

Real Fake News

The big news in the world today is fake news.

I know what you are thinking. How do I know *this* isn't fake news?

My answer to you is, of course it's fake news! That is why my newspaper column was always printed with a thick black border. It prevented leakage.

Fake news is all the rage. Thanks to that great big publisher in the sky called "the internet," people who never bothered to acquire a degree in journalism are typing the darnedest things on their laptops, tablets and smartwatches. Then they push the key that says "enter," and it becomes news.

As a result, other people are doing all kinds of crazy things. First of all, they're believing it. Then they press "share" to spread the fake news. The next thing you know, a guy is shooting up a pizzeria in Washington, D.C. because he got anchovies instead of pepperoni.

As a former pizzeria employee, I can attest that is a totally defensible crime. Our boss, Richard Jensen, would sometimes write up a fake pizza order with extra anchovies, just to test our decibel level.

Gotcha'! Rich really did make us holler, but the guy in D.C. actually shot up the pizzeria because of fake news. He'd read that it was the center of a child abuse ring, and was going to make it all better with his handgun and assault-style rifle.

I promise not to lie again for the duration of this piece. It erodes the trust between writer and reader, and detracts from the subject at hand: that fake news is bad, especially in a country where both firearms and anchovies are legalized.

The problem is, how do you tell the difference between fake and real news?

First, consider the source. Is your third-grade son telling you KFC burns the beaks off its chickens so they won't injure one another while waiting to become extra crispy? Yeah, that one turned us off KFC for a few weeks, before we finally figured out birds need their beaks to eat.

It was still early in the fake news game, and we were real rubes. Now we are seasoned skeptics, and ready to usher you on to your second warning signal: check the headline.

If it sounds outrageous, the story is probably fake. Years ago, our hometown newspaper ran a 100 percent true story headlined, "Car Hits Cow." Shortly after, Tonight Show host Jay Leno shared it in his *Real but Ridiculous Headlines from America's Newspapers* segment.

It was a real feather in our cap, and it was real news, but outrageous headlines that don't mention cows getting hit by cars should send up a red flag. If the story sounds fake, it quite likely is, unless there is a celebrity involved, in which case anything goes.

If you believe both the source and the headline, you are ready to clinch the deal. Confirm the so-called news with a reliable second opinion, preferably from a fourth grader or older. And if the story is surrounded by a thick black border? Gotcha' again!

Guerilla Artist Crosses Lines

Whenever I go shopping with our grandchildren, I keep them safely tucked into the cart so they won't grow up to be guerilla artists.

If you are a stranger to the genre, allow me to explain: I can't. All I can do is repeat what I've heard, about Carson Brown of Grand Rapids. He stacks stuff in store aisles, snaps a photo, then bolts for the exit. It's called "impromptu art."

And I think it warrants a time out, right after Carson has cleaned up his mess.

I heard all about it on National Public Radio, which is our major source of news with a minor in entertainment. We'd watch the local news on TV, but the channel only comes in when the leaves are down and our neighbor isn't running his tractor.

Carson Brown is a commercial photographer and artist. He goes into random big box department stores, gathers up a variety of objects that are all the same color, then stacks them in an aisle where they become impromptu art.

While they are still being art, and before management discovers it, Brown snaps a photo to post on his web page. Then he darts out the door, leaving shoppers scratching their heads at the color-coordinated road block in Aisle 6 that some poor stock boy is going to have to re-shelve.

When called to task (interviewed by an art magazine), Brown explained his work as "a response to overstimulation I felt in a retail environment." In his defense, he said it is done to "disrupt the visual landscape of consumerism."

He takes pride in his work, noting that he's been particularly artistic in a store near his home. The staff there has even taken to carrying walkie-talkies in an effort to nab him at his easel--I mean, "aisle." They haven't filled their Brown tag yet, but they've come mighty close.

As a card-carrying grandmother (AARP) (it's my husband's), I deal with overstimulation in a retail environment on a fairly regular basis. Someone who sounds like me asks, "Cookies?", the grandkids holler, "Chocolate chip!" and Gummi shifts into overdrive, taking the corners on two wheels.

Imagine what would happen if Brown got there first, to disrupt the visual landscape of consumerism. Gummi's reflexes aren't what they used to be. Impromptu art would fly. So might her grandchildren. Worst of all, chocolate chip cookies would crumble.

And what kind of world would it be if everybody ignored the rules and crossed the lines in their respective professions? No hands up? OK, Gummi's got this one too. It would be BAD.

Policemen would play tag with their tasers. Road crews would arrange traffic cones like mazes (wait--they already do!). Lawyers would argue with their mothers and win. Politicians would pretty much conduct business as usual.

And let's not even think about how loggers would successfully butt into long lines.

Call me old fashioned, but I think art has its place, and that's on the refrigerator door under a nice, stout magnet. Sculpture goes back in the Play-Doh containers so it doesn't dry out. And retail items need to stay neatly stacked on their shelves, right where they belong.

Unless they are chocolate chip cookies, which belong right in Gummi's cart.

Emmett always follows the Rules of the Road—especially when they lead to the cookie jar

Spa Bathrooms Waste Space

Q: What is a tranquil retreat that promotes good health and wellbeing while reducing stress?

A: Your Thomas Crapper.

Crapper was an English businessman and plumber who founded a sanitary equipment company in London in the 1800s. He is also the father of the U-bend plumbing trap, patented the floating ballcock, and received several royal warrants, including the Royal Flush.

I was being totally straight up until that poker reference. But if you were to ask me what is the most disturbing trend in home construction/renovation today, I would have to say people care way too much about Thomas's unfortunate namesake.

Ever since the outhouse found its way in, man has struggled to delicately define his waste space. He hasn't struggled too hard—a toilet, sink and tub with a *Field & Stream* within easy reach generally got the job done—but it was still a big step up from long walks and sharp slivers.

That was your basic bathroom. Your early fancy edition sported monogrammed towels, little pink soaps shaped like seashells that nobody was ever allowed to use, and an issue of *Good Housekeeping* thrown in for the Missus.

And that was just fine, because nobody especially cared to linger in the bathroom. Then along came the millennials, with their appreciation for comfort and design and the things in life that are even finer than little pink seashell soaps, and the spa-like bathroom was born.

A spa-like bathroom isn't a place where you just go. Well it kind of is, but you also go there to relax, unwind and pamper yourself while other family members try to beat the door down because they need to take care of business.

Of course, you can't just plug in an air freshener, pour some bath beads into the tub and call your Thomas good. A spa-like bathroom is an experience, one that must be carefully cultivated via the tasteful application of soothing elements. Like house plants.

House plants love the bathroom because it's the only place in the house where they can get a decent drink. Nobody remembers to water their plants, but everybody steams up the bathroom. House plants also add an element of nature, which is beneficial to people who spend too much time in the Thomas.

Natural wood is also key to spa-like bathroom living (again with the nature thing). You should use calming colors and scents, your tub should have claw feet, and you should blow your budget on blingy hardware, "treating your plumbing fixtures as jewelry."

You should also display fine art in your spa-like bathroom, if you can still afford it after purchasing your plumbing fixture jewelry. Finally, you should provide luxurious seating in your Thomas, even though the line is clearly formed outside of it.

If you're wondering just how you could fit a chaise lounge into your bathroom, you are still thinking small. Spa-like bathrooms are huge! You could park an Audi in a spa-like bathroom. A Chevy sedan would fit, too, but only pricey foreign models are allowed.

It's a Thomas Crapper thing.

Weather Poodle Alert

Forecasting lost a lot of its charm when weather poodles went out of fashion.

Weather poodles were small ceramic figurines coated with a clear chemical that worked like a barometer. Posted anywhere in the house but mostly on a coffee table, they turned pink during fair weather and blue during foul.

A weather poodle was the perfect gift for Mom. You could get one from the dime store for a song, then enjoy fiddling with it on blue days. When it broke, you just replaced it on the next Mom holiday, unless you had used up all her bath beads too, which cost even less than weather poodles.

Our grandma's weather poodle never got broken because it enjoyed limited exposure to bored children. It even had two poodle puppies, affixed to its collar with delicate gold chains. They were good little back-up systems because they were always the same color as their mom.

Forty-some years and many miles north later, I find U.P. weather fairly predictable. It's a blue poodle, with six months of snow and a month of cold rain on either end. The other four months are varying shades of pink poodle, with blue poodle undertones.

This year it was warm right up until Christmas, and it's been in the pink since. Cross country skiers are suffering from lack of grooming. Their slopes and trails aren't looking good, either. Snowmobilers have to trailer their sleds at high speeds because there's not enough snow to drive them that way.

If only we hadn't unleashed the weather poodles! This still would have happened, but at least we'd have something to play with. It may have been an inexact and downright kitschy science, but the poodles never lied, and neither did pieces of poodles.

When the fad finally ended, expedited I think by an industry that was just a bit threatened by all those cute canines, the public was left at the mercy of the elements. And because the elements in the U.P. have no mercy, it's anybody's guess.

Topping our personal weather forecasting arsenal is your classic outdoor thermometer, nailed to a deck rail. If it disappears, it's snowing. If that doesn't satisfy our need to know, we refer next to our indoor weather barometer.

It's a decorative blown-glass bulb with a thin spout, about half-filled with tinted water. When the water rises up the spout, it's high tide outside. When it spills out and onto my living room floor, there is a major disturbance indoors.

Our pets also tell us a lot about the weather. When the horse is standing in her shed with her head hung low, it's freezing and boring outside. When the dog comes inside and shakes, it's raining. When the cats are having a spat, could be anything. That's why you had your weather poodles instead of weather cats.

Less really is more, and the most memorable forecasters of all brought the sunshine no matter what the weather. Back when weather poodles still populated end tables, early TV weathermen didn't just tell you what the weather would bring. They drew pictures.

The TV weatherman of my childhood was armed only with a big blank sheet of paper and a black magic marker. He drew arrows to indicate wind patterns, slashes for sheets of rain, fluffy clouds for fluffy clouds and sunny faces for sunshine, usually south of the U.P.

He wasn't always right, but it was hard to hold a grudge against a guy who could create a panoramic vista from a barometer reading. I especially liked his hot weather forecast: a picture of a smiling sun sucking down a cold glass of lemonade.

It was art! It was science! It was a big, pink weather poodle with her two pink puppies, safely tucked away in memory.

From Mouths of Babes

Far be it from me to pick on innocent children participating in an industry devoted to helping consumers make informed decisions.

Yeah, that's far enough. What's with kids in advertising?

For the record, which I am currently typing at about 45 words per minute, children have always had a place in advertising. Traditionally, it was on the couch with the *Sears Wish Book* in their laps, circling toys they wanted for Christmas until their crayons ran out.

Later, it was perched in front of the TV, committing to memory every toy commercial that crossed the screen so they could ask for it later. If they were good little consumers, they could even sing the jingle for extra credit:

It's Slinky, it's Slinky, for fun it's a wonderful toy. It's Slinky, it's Slinky, it's fun for a girl or a boy.

Fifteen minutes into Christmas morning, you'd be crying over a sprung spring that wasn't fun for anyone, yet the catchy jingle remains deeply embedded in my brain. That is the problem with successfully helping consumers make informed decisions. It can cause brain damage.

Children have a place in front of the camera, too, but the product they're advertising should be age-appropriate, like sweetened cereal, or mac & cheese, or *"I wish I were an Oscar Mayer"* wieners. It shouldn't be the family's new sedan.

An automotive company that is leading the industry in annoying advertising recently ran a commercial in which real children, not actors, were asked what they liked about its cars. And because their residuals would cover their future college tuition, the kids piped right up.

They liked the roominess, the upholstery, the back-up camera and the dashboard's hidden storage space. One especially precocious child said she would store her dill pickle popcorn in it. She'll probably be able to swing a Ph.D.

Actually, the most disturbing thing about the commercial was not pickles in the storage space, though that was definitely a close second. It was the advertiser's assumption that consumers care about what kids want in a car.

Back when a Slinky was considered cutting-edge technology, parents couldn't have cared less about their children's riding comfort. Too hot? Roll down your window. Bored? Count cows. Your brother got left back at the gas station? We're baby boomers! We'll just make another one!

If boomer babies complained about the car upholstery, they'd get left behind on purpose.

Advertisers see it differently, probably because children are cuter than actual experts. That is why kids whose tool boxes were made by Mattel are hawking auto repair, metal roofs and well drilling—which they pretend to do themselves while wearing Fischer Price safety glasses and hard hats.

Children want us to buy a boat cruise, a friends & family calling plan and a visit to California, the Dreamers State. Before you know it, they'll be working for the really big bucks, playing doctor on TV and dispensing advice on what pills we need to take so we can keep up the carpool.

As long as our car sports plenty of room and a nice back-up camera, for retrieving the little advertiser we left behind at the gas station.

11. DEALING WITH WHEELING

Road Gators Bite

I recently reported, proud as punch, that Michigan is a cobra-free state.

Now I find there are road gators lurking around almost every turn.

I learned all about it from the Allstate Blog, which "offers everyday peace of mind through tips and education about safety, preparedness, maintenance and more," even though they are an insurance company which would greatly benefit from our not listening.

For the record, which I will soon have if I keep picking on major corporations, road gators are long strips of rubber than have torn off truck tires and are now sunning their steel-reinforced backs on our roadways, just waiting to take a bite out of your car.

Like actual alligators, road gators can run about eight to ten feet long. Unlike real alligators, which can top out at over 900 pounds (1,100 if they have recently ingested a tourist), road gators average about 70 pounds, and lose weight with each successive hit.

Every year, road gators are responsible for an unknown number of accidents in Michigan, because nobody wants to admit they got sucker-slapped by a tire tread. They "slice open oil pans, rip off steering components and smash through windshields."

They are a full-length action feature, just waiting to happen!

People like to lay the blame on retreads and capped tires. Studies by persons who spend way too much time with ruined rubber indicate full-size road gators are the progeny of "virgin" truck tires, which is a very clever way to get people to read a boring report.

Apparently, you can tell the difference in the wild by looking at the road gator as you carefully swerve around it, engaging the kiddies if they aren't too busy fighting in the back seat. Smooth edges? Retread. Ragged edges? Immaculate conception!

Most tires fail due to human error. We underinflate them. We use them to find the curb. We drive on them across Pure Michigan, which is Pure Potholes due to our long winters and short budgets.

Keeping with its promise to keep our minds at peace, Allstate offers some helpful tips on how to avoid future road gator bites in Michigan. Some are even included in the following. See if you can tell the difference!

- First, look ahead of you, because believe you me, gators on the road are a lot less disturbing than whatever the kids are doing in the back seat.

- Next, if you do see bits of black rubber on the road, holler "Retread!" and win the game.

- Slow down, because nobody is a winner if the gator has its way, except for a large corporation.

- Michiganders don't "veer for deer," and we don't "cater to the gator." If you can't safely maneuver around a road gator, run right over it and hope for the best. The drivers on either side of you will thank you. So will their insurance companies.

- Finally, if you are driving beside a big rig and hear a telltale "whap-whap-whap," loudly remind the children that rap is not music, and they are ruining their hearing. If the noise continues, slow down, because a road gator is about to be born.

Aren't you glad we don't have cobras?

Caroling Car on a Roll

I enjoy listening to National Public Radio (NPR) on Saturday mornings, when it interrupts its regular, socially responsible, a-little-heavy-on-the-classical-music programming to broadcast *Car Talk*.

The show's hosts are Tom and Ray Magliozzi, alias "Click and Clack, the Tappet Brothers." They take calls on car problems, then offer a diagnosis and cure, right over the airwaves. Sometimes it's as simple as replacing a belt. Other times, it involves a wrecker.

In our mobile society, people's lives and car troubles often become intertwined. That's when Click and Clack truly shine, doling out sensitive marital advice along with loud laughter, occasional snorts and liberal doses of the word, "divorce."

Only Click and Clack pronounce it "divaws," because they are from Boston. It makes NPR all the more appealing to the masses.

My favorite part of the show is the noises callers often make to describe their car problems. With hardly any prompting at all, they let loose with a stream of sick engine sounds that would make a classical music fan sit up and say, "Ah! Chopin's 4th in E Rectitude! Though a tad heavy on the percussion..."

Personally, I have no call to call on the Tappet Brothers for advice. There are exactly two undesirable noises my car makes, and I am all too familiar with the causes. "Thup-thup" means I have a rock in my tire. "Thunk" means I have a deer in my grill.

If I call a major airwave with a car concern, you can bet I am going to make the most of my dime. I'd give Click and Clack an earful by repeating the noise my car starts making every year, starting in November, as soon as I turn the key:

Chestnuts roasting on an open fire, Jack Frost nipping at your nose...

That's right. When I turn on my car, Mel Torme pours out. Not literally, because Mel didn't go "thunk" first. No, Mel comes out, along with Bing Crosby and Perry Como and Frank Sinatra because:

It's the most wonderful time of the year!

I have an unnatural affection for Christmas music. I like it so much, I have been playing it since early November, but only on cloudy days suggestive of snow. And on rainy days that look like melting snow. On sunny days I pout and listen to country.

I trace the affection way back to kindergarten, when my favorite song, right after "A Horse is a Horse of Course of Course," was "Silent Night." At my near-daily request, Miss Haberichter would settle onto her piano bench with a loud sigh, and plunk along as I crooned for my classmates.

Funny, but I don't recall ever hearing a word about class reunions.

No matter, because nowadays I can get my fix on the road. My car is fully loaded with Christmas CDs, and I am not afraid to use them. Just ask our children, who blessedly failed to inherit Mom's crooning gene but can't escape her Caroling Car.

The Caroling Car was my good ol' Toyota Rav 4, a box on wheels in a shade of mint green that looked like last year's gum drops. The children barely noticed it until their teen years, especially their teen years during the months of November and December. By then, there was no escaping it.

You know how it is. You drive to school to pick up your daughter from volleyball practice. She finishes a half hour late, comes strolling out of the gym, then stops to have a leisurely chat with her friends before the long, boring drive home with Mom.

That's when the Caroling Car would mysteriously come to life. The two front windows would slowly roll down, the radio volume knob would spin like a top, and the spirit of Christmas would ring out across the parking lot:

DING DONG MERRILY ON HIGH, IN HEAV'N THE BELLS ARE RING-ING!

The mortified teen would come rocketing to the car, slamming against the passenger door in her haste to stop the music. I'd hint at a donation for gas—it was Christmas, after all—but would settle for the gift of the child, even though she switched out my Bing Crosby CD for heavy metal.

I have a new, blue Caroling Car this year. It's harder to share my love of Christmas music with the kids now that they're grown, but I'm sure a guest stint on NPR would reach out and touch at least one of them, preferably the volleyball player who dented my door.

I'd call in about some random car noise, and with the Tappet Brothers' blessing, would tip my head back and start right in on "Silent Night." As my lovely strains spread out across the land, somewhere a classical music fan who was spinning his radio dial would pause and say:

"Muffler sounds shot on that clunker—and why do I suddenly feel like I'm back in kindergarten?"

"Dusty Rose" Hits the Trail

Sometimes it is not enough to kick up your feet, mop up the coffee you just spilled, call a couple sources and knock out a story for your hometown newspaper.

Sometimes, you have to be in the trenches. I mean, "arroyos."

You read me right. Last winter, I wrote a gripping piece about snowbirds--Yoopers who winter in warmer climes--from the comfort of my desk. Last week, the newspaper reluctantly cut me loose (held the door open) (I think I felt a slight shove) for a follow-up in sunny Tucson, AZ.

Nancy and Mike Lewis enjoy a well-deserved break from hosting "Dusty Rose"

It is the land of the majestic saguaro cactus and many lesser cacti, all heavily needled. It is also the home of friends Mike and Nancy Lewis, of snowbird fame. In spite of the story, they opened their home and their lawn chairs for my husband and me. All we had to do was hop on a few airplanes to get there.

Modern air travel is a marvel of mankind. You pay an exorbitant fee to be unshod, scanned, then ferried aloft in a tight cylinder. The terms for your release are constantly changing until your airplane spits you out again, ideally but not necessarily at your intended destination.

Can you tell someone nearly got bumped on an overbooked flight, got lucky on stand-by after another flight was delayed for seven hours, then had to sprint through O'Hare like a fallen former football player to catch the last leg of her journey on a puddle jumper to Ironwood?

I didn't think so. Discretion is the mark of the true professional.

We landed in Tucson after dark, but quickly saw the light. We had left the U.P. early that morning in heavy snow and three degrees. The snow banks were higher than our car. In Tucson, it was almost 60 degrees. Mike and Nancy apologized for the unseasonable chill.

Their community is surrounded by desert. A neighbor has been making inroads, creating meandering paths marked by stones painted green or white. You're welcome to stray if you like, but there are no shortcuts on the cactus-studded terrain that's always on defense.

We visited Saguaro National Park, home of the giant saguaro cactus, "universal symbol of the American West." Saguaros are protected, can grow to over 50 feet tall and can live for 150-200 years. They sprout branches, or arms, after about 100 years. Mike and Nancy have a baby one out front.

The next day we hit the Arizona-Sonora Desert Museum to see animals, exhibits, and meat-eating birds flying perilously close overhead. It's the Raptor Free Flight! The live show features large raptors on the wing, released to fly over Desert Museum guests and land on nearby perches heavily baited with meat. Along their way, visitors are welcome to take pictures, and strongly encouraged to duck.

Volunteers warn against raising hands, cameras or small children due to low-flying air traffic. When a huge hawk overhead made a beeline for the bait, I could feel the wind from the beating of its wings. A tall man in the crowd proudly stated he gets tagged on a regular basis.

Of course, any journalist worth her salt prepares exhaustively for an assignment of this magnitude. I checked the box by lucking into a collection of Louis L'Amour Westerns at the local thrift shop just before we left town.

The Shadow Riders escorted me out West, and *The Key-Lock Man* saw me back up North. In between, I made it my personal goal to use every Western phrase I'd read as I hiked, ducked, and sweated my way across the Lewis's turf in Tucson.

A leashed dog that lunged at me was a bad hombre. The bee that stung my husband on a hike was a dry-gulcher. And when Mike said he had to use a pickaxe to break up the dirt outside their house in order to plant their baby saguaro, I was first on the draw: "Sod buster!"

But I am even worse than a sod buster, because like a tenderfoot, I failed to pack my ChapStick for a trip to the wild West. In the desert heat, I had to resort instead to using lipstick round-the-clock. I left town as a reporter, but returned as a painted lady who's still packing her hue with pride.

"Dusty Rose" is back in town.

Where's the Grease?

The tension in the waiting room was palpable.

When the door finally opened, a man in a gleaming white shirt and khakis emerged, and summoned a woman to the front. Our hearts went with her, then skipped a collective beat at the terrible news, delivered in an appropriately somber tone:

"I'm sorry. It's your transmission--and your warranty is up."

If you are old enough to remember cans of motor oil opened with a metal spout, then poured into your engine by a guy in greasy coveralls, when is our next class reunion? And when did the auto industry go all Marcus Welby, M.D.?

Welby was the beloved star of a 1970s TV show. Unlike your modern-day TV docs, who spill more blood performing a tonsillectomy than both sides did at Antietam, Welby was concerned and caring, curing his patients without even wrinkling his lab coat.

And that, my dear friends, is the problem with modern garages. They need to get the grease out.

When I walk into a modern garage in search of a repair, I have to wipe my feet first, take care not to sit in the area wired for people with attachments, then surrender a kidney as security before I can hand over my car keys.

(Just joshing about the kidney. No way would that cover a new transmission. A liver, maybe, but mine's been to too many Fish Camps.)

There are waiting rooms for the customers' comfort. Floors sparkle, chairs are upholstered, and the magazines are all in good taste. There's hot coffee, water and pop in the fridge, and even fresh-baked cookies if the salesmen haven't gotten to them first.

The area where mechanics actually work on your car isn't even visible. Neither are the mechanics. They're not even allowed to come out for cookies. And because I've been a car owner since the 1980s, it all kind of makes me squirm, despite the cozy seating.

Until a few short weeks ago, when I finally saw the light.

It was the sun, and it was baking me to a crisp inside our 2007 Toyota Corolla because the air conditioner had quit. Burning with impulse, I turned into a local garage, was rewarded with an opening in the schedule, and shown to the waiting room.

Actually, nobody showed it to me. I just kind of plopped down onto a dusty seat across from the counter, facing the working man's bathroom, and basked in the glory of what a garage ought to be.

The floor was worn by people who never wipe their feet. So was the working man's bathroom. So was my chair, upholstered in cracked brown Naugahyde. Even though it scratched the backs of my legs, I knew I'd landed well.

Shelves on the walls were loaded with junk and coated in dust. If I got bored with the view, I could watch the mechanic working on my car through the open garage door. If I needed cookies, there was a store down the street, and if I needed a bathroom, I could probably wait until I got home.

Time flew while I was having fun. Finally, a man in grease-smudged coveralls delivered the diagnosis, right across the counter, loud and clear and with a friendly grin that assured me he had about as much use for my kidney as he did for my Corolla.

"It's your pump. How many miles you got on that car? Summers are short. Roll down yer' window."

There ought to be a TV show.

Dirty Driving

If I am ever stopped by a traffic cop, there is at least one citation I'm not going to be able to talk my way out of: Operating a Landfill Without a License.

It's not that big a deal. I could probably make bail with the spare change stuck between my seats. But every time I come to a stop, causing two McDonald's coffee cups, a volleyball and a window scraper to roll underfoot, I resolve anew to get the kids to clean out my car.

The problem is, I reside in my car. I don't live in my car because I am a victim of poverty in America. I live in my car because I have three children in sports.

Sports keep children off the streets, and parents on the road. When my husband and I escaped the urban sprawl of L'Anse to settle in Watton, we didn't realize we'd be returning some days (twice the other days), to keep our kids off the streets, even though most of them aren't even paved.

It all started in a gym far away--in the U.P., every gym is far away-- when some unsupervised child rolled her basketball right in front of our daughter. Katy picked it up, smiled wide, and said those words that would forever change both our lives and driving patterns:

"I want to participate in junior high ball! And compete against schools in different time zones! And practice in town every night of the week! Including Saturdays!"

Once word got out, there was no stopping her two siblings from following suit. We've lived the life of Nomads ever since, moving from one sport to the next, eating, drinking, napping and accumulating car clutter as we wait for one child or another to emerge from a gym.

It would be petty and small of me to blame my car's sorry interior upon our sports-loving kids. I blame their little friends, too, whose empty juice boxes, candy wrappers, and sneakers occasionally rise to the surface in the car that I call home.

With all due respect to my own parents, they raised me better. Unfortunately, they also allowed me to ride in my brothers' vehicles.

Jim taught me to always get coffee with your gas, and never throw away the cup. I developed an addiction to strong coffee and an immunity to clutter. Both served me well when Jim joined the Air Force and left me his '69 Chrysler Newport, fully loaded.

If Jim was bad, Mark was worse. The back seat of Mark's black T-Bird was home to White Castle hamburger boxes, jumper cables and Boy Scout equipment he was still hauling around since his last campout, which was roughly eight years ago.

We never got in trouble for car clutter. Our folks figured, "You made your mess, now drive in it." But Mark came closest to having to clean up his act after Dad nearly got scalped while riding shotgun.

Mark's friend, Greg Skerkiewicz, had snuck into his car earlier that day, and removed the bolts from his passenger seat as a joke. Later on, Dad and Mark were headed in the same direction, probably White Castle for more burgers, so Dad hopped a ride with his son.

Mark pulled away from the curb kind of quickly, as young T-Bird drivers are wont to do. Safely buckled into his unbolted passenger seat, Dad tipped over backward, landing with his feet in the air and his nose mere inches from the business end of Mark's Boy Scout hatchet.

I may operate a motorized landfill, but you can rest assured I allow neither hatchets nor Greg Skerkiewicz in my car. My car is my home, and my word is law: always be sure to check your seat bolts before I pull away from the curb.

Ready, Set, Mow!

What do Sodzilla, the Turfinator and Mr. Mowjangles all have in common?

If you answered, "They grappled with Mothra in a grade-B Japanese movie!", you lose, but not by much. The three mentioned above, and the Prograsstinator too, are all stars of the wildly popular sport of lawnmower racing.

I learned all about it by tuning into the national news last weekend. Because most national news occurs during the week, weekend newscasters are forced to come up with lively features to keep their viewers engaged between bass fishing shows.

They usually cook up something with a famous chef, taking a bite just before the commercial break so they can spit it out off-camera. You can't be a national newscaster and eat, too. It softens the facial planes.

The newscasters must have finally succeeded in offending every chef in town, because last weekend they were forced to stage a race. It was a lawnmower race. They raced around hay bales. For this, their parents paid good money for journalism school.

Dressed in NASCAR-style garb, a team of newscasters interviewed a member of the U.S. Lawnmower Racing Association, or USLMRA for slightly shorter. I don't recall precisely what he said because it wasn't about bass fishing, but the gist was, racing-style lawnmowers go really fast.

Armed with that valuable insight, the newscasters pulled their starter cords, and were off! They drove on an oval track ringed by hay bales and New Yorkers who had never seen a real, live lawnmower. A few tentatively held out handfuls of hay as they sped by, but the lawnmowers weren't hungry.

Cutting to slightly later that day, I researched the not-so-new sport in a more sensible manner. I played a game of solitaire, Googled "lawnmower racing," then took a cookie break because print journalists don't have to worry about facial planes.

When I returned, I learned the organization was founded on April Fool's Day in 1992. The very first USLMRA race was held the following month, on Labor Day weekend.

It was kind of a joke, but when you mix men and fast lawnmowers, it's bound to spark major interest. A new sport was born, with a potentially practical side too, all thanks to USLMRA chapters across the nation and their sponsors, including STA-BIL and Chia Pet.

Drivers compete throughout the U.S., in track classes for machines geared up to 60 mph. Unsullied by money, the racers instead reap their rewards in gleaming trophies and bragging rights:

"I drive a lawnmower! Really, really fast!"

Just because some print people have a problem with glamorous sports, that's no reason to be turned off by the wonderful world of lawnmower racing. Instead, you should be turned off by the couple who met on the track, then returned before a big race to exchange their marital vows.

The wedding of the lawnmower racing season took place last Labor Day in Mansfield, OH. The groom wore a green sequined jacket and had green accents in his hair. The bride was decked out in a faux grass dress. She was given in marriage by her dad, who drives his lawnmower too fast, too.

The big news here is not that a bride finally dressed worse than her bridesmaids, or that the groom didn't get mowed down for showing up at a USLMRA event in sequins. The big news is, "all cutting blades are removed for safety."

A lawnmower without a blade? What is the point of a legion of mowers crossing great, grassy plains if they can't leave a neatly groomed landscape behind them? It's not lawnmowing—it's lawngoing!

Back to those racy newscasters, the lady reporter was in the lead most of the way, and then a fellow journalist started to pull ahead. Coming into a turn, he literally hit the hay, causing great concern among fellow New Yorkers who ran to get a vet for his mount.

His mower was loaded for bear, but couldn't chew its way out of the grass, so the lady won. She jumped for joy. Mr. Mow It All beamed. I'm still pulling for Mothra.

12. FEAR IS WHY WE'RE HERE

My Computer is Dying!

When my computer recently died, a part of me died with it. It was the part that understood how to use my computer.

It happened just a short while back. I got up in the morning, switched on my laptop to see who was misbehaving on Facebook, and my screen went all dark and ominous with the warning, "The sky is falling! The sky is falling!"

Wait. That's Chicken Little. My screen said, "Your hard drive is failing! Your hard drive is failing!" Unlike the misfortunate little bird that was hit on the head by a falling apple, I'd been dealt a life-changing blow by a laptop.

The problem is not so much the computer as my utter unwillingness to evolve. In the course of human history, every age has been marked by man's ability to embrace change. And then there are the rest of us.

"Wheel, schlemiel."

"Man wasn't meant to fly."

"My hard drive is failing! My hard drive is failing!"

You catch my drift. I extended a shaky finger toward the light, and switched off my computer. Then I switched it on again, and the message hadn't changed. Then I ran and called our daughter for help, on our landline of course because we don't do that cell phone voodoo.

Katy assists her mother in times of technological crises, and was very reassuring. She said she would try to make the bad go away. In the meantime, I could use her laptop to write important stories and check to see who was in what bar last night.

I like my daughter's laptop, because her screen saver is a photo of our granddaughter. I was admiring it that very night when my daughter called to say that yes, indeed, my sky had fallen. I would have to pick up the pieces and have a new hard drive installed.

My life as I knew it has not been the same since.

My computer works great. The problem is that its operator is a Neanderthal (with apologies to the Neanderthals, who in times of crisis probably clubbed one another on the heads and grunted, "You are a Nancy Besonen!").

The computer came back with a new and improved operating system because in the wonderful world of technology, progress is good. My problem, and I understand I am not the only Neanderthal in Baraga County, is that progress is confusing.

Imagine taking your car in to have it serviced. When you get it back, the steering wheel is now located on the driver's door panel, the gas pedal is in the glove compartment and your rearview mirror is where you used to park your coffee cup.

And it's still easier to operate than your new operating system!

The new, improved system made me hunt for my email. If I didn't type nicely, it would not let me in. It also didn't get along with my previous version of Word Perfect, which I used to write my stories. It let me type them, but refused to save them.

All of a sudden, I had a computer with good taste.

And I could live with all that, but when the computer refused to download photos of my grandkids, it finally got the boot. I drove it back to the tech expert at Baraga Telephone, who is surely earning his eternal reward by dealing with the likes of me, and asked him to please restore my dated operating system.

It's good to be back in the Stone Age again. See you on Facebook!

Revenge of the Refrigerator

I have a problem with exaggeration, especially when someone who is usually me brings up the subject of fishing, but I am spot-on in warning that: Appliances are Taking Over the World!

The threat is real, as you can tell by the capitalized letters and exclamation mark, though exclamation marks have lost a lot of impact due to social media ("LOVE this chicken casserole!!!"). I'd have capitalized the entire sentence, but should probably save that for when the appliances actually succeed at world domination.

I learned all about it as I learn about most things these days, on my butt on the couch, staring at my laptop screen. I'm not worried about my laptop taking over the world because its battery is so old, it only works when I plug it in. I may not be a military mastermind, but even I know enough to unplug the enemy.

Appliances may come and go, but clotheslines are forever

The problem with The Dominator is, we can't unplug it because it holds everything that is near and dear to us, including the chicken we'll need for that casserole. That's right. The Dominator is the fridge.

At this very moment, your refrigerator could be playing you like a fiddle thanks to a new gizmo that connects you to the fridge via cameras, a screen, and your smartphone. Of course you are in control! Just like those scientists were at the start of *Jurassic Park*!

(Insert evil laugh here, sounds like MMMWOAHAHAHA!)

Again, evil laughter totally credits an exclamation mark at the end. And if there's one takeaway from the movie, it's that whenever you put your trust in technology, you're going to find yourself running for your life with a T-Rex snapping at your heels.

The cameras inside your fridge keep watch over your leftovers. The video screen on the door lets you plan meals, create calendars and watch your favorite movies. Your smartphone keeps the two of you in touch so you can visit any time with your new BFF, Best Fridge Forever.

From what I can gather on my butt on the couch, it is a perfect world, where smart refrigerators and dumb humans who can't even shop for groceries without calling the fridge from the store ("Do I need milk?"), live in perfect harmony.

Then one day, there's a little glitch in the system. You've seen a glitch: it's the iceberg in *The Titanic;* the emission software in VW's; a disagreement between you and your fridge about whether or not the leftover chicken salad is still safe.

Then suddenly, your refrigerator goes rogue.

The cameras inside it quit monitoring your food and turn on each other instead, resulting in an endless stream of fridge selfies that go viral on Facebook. The screen on the refrigerator door, which also turns out to be a real wiseacre, plans family meals starring expired eggs.

The calendar option is filled with family outings to home centers. The only reminder you can bring up on the fridge screen is a flashing "CLEAN ME!", and its on-screen entertainment consists entirely of Maytag commercials.

Appliances love the Maytag Man.

And how, you ask, can we protect ourselves? Well, it's obviously too late to not read this. Regarding world domination by your appliances, keep an eye on the fridge, a hand on the cord, and be sure to tune in again next week for "Massage Chair Massacre."

Cobras Can't Touch Us

As the search continues for an escaped cobra in Florida, we can all thank our lucky stars we live in Michigan.

I've been following the story for a week now, even though it pretty much petered out after three days. The snake is a tan and yellow monocled cobra, among the deadliest in the world, and is currently slithering, free as you please, through the Great Snake State.

The fugitive got loose when an apprentice snake handler opened the lid on the cobra's cage, apparently to confirm there was an actual cobra inside. When it popped up to greet him with a great big smile, the apprentice hastily left the premises.

In the words of our own former world leader, "Yer' fired!"

Although the apprentice carefully closed the door behind him, the monocled cobra (whose name summons the bumbling Colonel Klink on *Hogan's Heroes,* which kind of dilutes the threat), somehow managed to escape. And Florida responded accordingly.

Officials urged residents to use caution, neighbors called around, and some joker created a Twitter account for the snake announcing,

"Finally free!" An obese lizard was also x-rayed to see if it had a cobra inside, but the results were inconclusive.

"You're worried about someone breaking in and robbing you, and now you're going to worry about a snake if you step out going to work," said a concerned neighbor. "That's scary."

If you are wondering what possible connection this snake story has to our own Great Lakes State, you clearly have not gone the distance on US-41. The highway that begins in Copper Harbor, MI ends in Miami, FL, resulting in a direct link with the Great Snake State!

I learned all about it on a vacation in Florida, where our family visited friend and former co-worker Rick Buck. Buck met us at the airport, decked out in pants sporting a chili pepper print. After we convinced the kids that Buck was safe, he led our rental car a merry chase to his home in Port Charlotte.

Buck wasn't afraid of snakes, because he'd already been vaccinated. An Army brat, Buck was bitten by a rattlesnake while riding his bicycle on base as a kid. He lost his calf muscle in the aftermath, and almost his leg. After recovering from the chili pants, our kids couldn't get enough of Buck.

His old injury didn't slow Buck down one bit, either, and my husband struggled to keep up in our rental car. All of a sudden, thankfully at a red light, Buck popped out of his car in front of us and began wildly pointing to a sign alongside the highway. It read, "End East US-41."

Copper Harbor makes a much bigger splash at the start of the highway, with an ornate wooden sign that includes information about Indian footpaths and fur traders and such, but people there have a lot more time to read it. And by the way, the distance between that sign and the one in Miami is exactly 1,990 miles.

The good news, for Michiganders at least, is there are eight states between us and Cobra Klink. Back in 2015, a cobra named Elvis that escaped its enclosure in Florida was found a little over a month later, when a neighbor was loading her dryer and heard a hissing sound.

Personally, I can't see Klink slithering past Tennessee.

We may have slush and snow in March, and we'll probably have it in April and sometimes May, but here in Pure Michigan we can golf without checking for 'gators, load our dryers without worrying if Elvis has left the building, and safely step outside to go to work in the morning.

As long as we remember to put on our snow boots first.

Reporters are Replaceable

There is a disturbing trend in the news world these days, almost as disturbing as the news itself but not quite there yet: putting journalists in death-defying situations for entertainment's sake.

A short while ago, I turned on the TV and saw Ann Curry, a reporter on the NBC morning news, talking about a charity sponsored by the station. If viewers sent in just $10,000, they could, figuratively speaking, tip her right into oblivion.

It seems that Ann, probably under the influence of too much morning coffee, had foolishly shared an interest in bungee jumping with someone in the ratings department. Before you could say, "Go jump off a bridge," Ann was preparing to go jump off a bridge.

Ratings rose into the stratosphere as the network rabidly advertised her leap of faith. Money came pouring in, and suddenly, there was Ann, perched precariously atop a high bridge in England with rubber cords strapped to her sides.

Then she jumped, or maybe her producer pushed her, and as she plummeted towards the Motherland, riveted viewers from around the world could hear Ann's plaintive cry: "WHY DIDN'T I MAJOR IN MAAATTTTHHHHH?"

I'd have to agree with Ann. The last time I trusted a bungee cord, I was chased halfway down our basement stairs and pinned against the wall by a washing machine. You can't trust those bungee cords; or washing machines you've been overloading for the past 20 years, either.

Ann is not the only journalist seriously regretting her undergraduate choices. I have seen newscasters buckled into speeding NASCARs, and wedged into rocketing toboggans in varying shades of green--the reporters, not their vehicles.

They send reporters up in airplanes that fly so fast you float, and strap them onto snowboards atop icy Alpine slopes for stories about the crazy things people do. It's both Nature's and the networks' way of keeping the journalist population in check.

Closer to home, TV news reporters with no hunting experience whatsoever have been armed and sent out into the field after wild game. They didn't see any, or maybe they just looked the other way, but the threat was real because those shotguns sure can kick.

Almost every winter, a TV news reporter lacking in seniority is assigned to dive into Lake Superior for a report on flotation suits for ice fishermen. The suits work fine--seasoned anglers who suddenly became bobbers wouldn't even stop fishing--but they ought to pick their reporters based on R-value.

The undersized reporter who surfaced last year was so cold, he couldn't even report. His mouth was working but no sound came out, which was probably good because it appeared to be saying a very bad word.

There used to be a job title for journalists seeking thrills and danger. It was "war correspondent." There are still war correspondents on the job. The rest of us are being sent into battle armed with college degrees, notepads and pens that skip. They skip because we're shaking.

The problem with this new and dynamic journalism is, we trained for it behind a keyboard. Reporters and newscasters are made of the write stuff. We love to write about the scary and exciting things other people do, then shut off our computers and nod off in our office chairs that conveniently recline.

If we recline too far, they tip over backward. It's the chance we take.

I must admit that sometimes, usually after I've tipped too far, I can see myself in one of those grand journalism moments, poised on the precipice of fame. I'm teetering atop the Bishop Baraga statue that towers over Keweenaw Bay, sporting an assortment of gently used bungee cords found on Pure Potholed Michigan's roadways.

Then the Bishop sneezes I think, because suddenly I'm toppling into space with bungees popping apart and raining down around me. Before you know it, I'm swimmin' with the fishes, while up above the crowd gleefully gathers up the spoils of my final report.

"I love these bungee things—they're great for moving heavy appliances!"

Data Thief Disappointment

A little-known Florida company may have exposed personal data of nearly every American.

A few short years ago, an announcement like that would have struck fear into the hearts of Americans everywhere, but mostly in America. We feel very strongly about our personal data. We don't want anybody to know anything about us, unless they are one of our 438 friends on Facebook.

According to the report, the possible leak involved almost two terabytes of data, containing nearly 340 million individuals' records. Our credit card and social security numbers are still safe, but our addresses and phone numbers, not so much.

I know what you are thinking, because I am thinking the same thing: "Is there still some of that Mexican fruit cake in the fridge?" Also, "Big deal! You can find my address and phone number right in the telephone book!"

Au contraire, I type in perfect French thanks to Google, because thanks to modern technology, hardly anybody's postal address and phone number is in the telephone book anymore. They're all stored in other people's cell phones. And in a little-known Florida company.

If I don't have someone's cell phone number, I have been known to look up a stranger in the phone book with the same last name, and hope they are (a) a relative, and (b) on speaking terms with the person I'm looking for. I am batting about .500. Strikeouts can be brutal, but colorful.

What makes the data breach even more frightening is that 400 of our personal, private characteristics may also be fully exposed. The computing criminal element may, at this very moment, be tuning into the facts that you are a smoker and a dog owner.

What are they going to do? Sniff you out and steal your dog?

The real problem with leaked data is that it could be used to profile you. The problem with that problem is, as a consumer, you are already being profiled all the time!

For instance, I use my computer to research important issues, like bananas on boats, Rogers Cinema and Bike Week in Sturgis, SD. This in turn causes it to feed me a steady diet of sunscreen ads, popular film trailers and images of women who do not dress with safety in mind while motorcycling.

In recent years, we have received a handful of notices informing us that our personal data may have been breached, and is in danger of seriously boring a hacker somewhere. The notices include the email address of a company that will help us out, free of charge, thereby exposing even more of our personal data for our own protection.

While they are waiting to hear all about us, I would like to take this opportunity to avoid a similar disaster at the keyboards of those dirty personal data stealers. That's right, I'm going to sing like a canary, spilling the truth and beating the bad guys to the draw:

I do not smoke.

I do not own a dog.

I do not need more sunscreen.

But I could sure use a little more of that Mexican fruit cake.

Fear is our Friend

It seems like only yesterday when smiley faces were rearing their ugly little heads everywhere, from tee shirts to coffee mugs to the dots on "i's" by people with way too much time on their hands. They carried with them a message that refuses to die: Have a Nice Day!

Now there's an even worse logo making the rounds: NO FEAR. My keyboard fails to do it justice because the words look like they're slashed in blood, a substance people with no fear tend to see a lot of, but they should still Have a Nice Day!

Fear, my friends, is why we're here. Back in prehistoric times, when dinosaur mothers warned their young, "Put your sweater on before you go play! It's an Ice Age out there!", what did those big, green, scaley kids reply? "NO FEAR."

A few short millenia later, when one caveman warned another, "Grog, you keep walking in that upright position and fashioning tools, you'll be paying off a big mortgage some day!", what did Grog reply? "NO FEAR."

Well, maybe that's actually why we're here. But as long as we are and if we care to stay, we need to remember that fear is our friend. It teaches us not to crawl into coffee tables, not to wash the cat, and not to call our big brother his family nickname, "Hinky Dinky Do," in front of his buddies.

The problem with NO FEAR is, it appeals to our sense of adventure, which isn't always sensible. Advertisers hire actors with NO FEAR to up the excitement factor of family sedans and cans of soda pop. It makes for a strong case against both drinking and driving:

- They race to the edge of a cliff to show how well the car stops.

- They skateboard upside down to prove the pop is heavily caffeinated.

- They let go of the steering wheel to clap along with the radio.

If you are like me--buying your brakes on the cheap, avoiding skateboarding altogether because it's just silly at age 65, and refusing to play patty cake at 60 mph--you, too, are living the life of FEAR. Long may we run from danger!

The good news is, FEAR never fails us. Nowadays, it keeps my knee pads from getting dirty when I play volleyball because I call balls that aren't coming directly to me: "That's yours!" "Yup, get that one too!" "DIVE!"

FEAR makes me strap on my bike helmet, step into my ice grips, warn tiny grandchildren to chew every bite (sometimes with a disturbing visual included) and never drive with teenagers unless I get to pick the music.

There are times in life when you just have to swallow your fear, no matter how bad it tastes. I took the gulp but not the hit the day I found myself between a rock and a hard place: a logging truck and a pickup.

We were all in a row, waiting to turn onto US-41, when the fully loaded logging truck in front of me suddenly started to back up, and the pickup truck behind me didn't.

I doubted the logger could even see my little red Toyota. He probably wouldn't even know I'd been harvested until he got to the sawmill and realized his mud flaps didn't match.

So, I beeped my horn as loud as I could.

The pickup finally backed up, and I did too, and I lived to type about it. A short way down the road I floored my gas pedal, and as I passed the logging truck at a zippy 45 mph (all that beeping took a lot out of my Toyota), I spotted a familiar decal on the driver's back window: NO FEAR.

I have just one thing to say to a person like that: Have a Nice Day!

13. PUTTING THE MISS IN CHRISTMAS

Just Use Money!

I would like to propose a radical idea that would make this Christmas shopping season the smoothest ever.

Just use money!

Back when real men wore wigs, our fathers brought forth on this continent real currency. And a lot of them put their own pictures on it. And for many score after, things ran pretty smoothly, especially if you had lots of their pictures in your pocket.

Then one day, someone whose head was a little too big for his wig proposed a better idea: using a credit card with nobody's head on it (major warning sign) to purchase things now and pay shortly after, or be thrown into debtor's prison.

Before you knew it, debtor's prisons dotted the land, and people still using credit cards were having their rear ends scanned by electronic pickpockets. Then America struck back, with lead-lined wallets that cause unsightly bulges but preserve our right to overspend.

It is a right we will not give up until they pry our credit cards from our cold, dead fingers.

People love to pay with plastic. They pay with credit cards, debit cards, gift cards and refund cards. Instead of handing over a fistful of dollars, which possibly bear traces of out-of-control substances but, by gosh, were good enough for our forefathers, they prefer to shuffle the deck.

After carefully choosing a card, they swipe it. Then they swipe it again, because it was upside down. Then they go for three because the baby got into their wallet and was teething on their credit cards.

The card finally wins the stand-off. The scanner retaliates by requesting more information. The purchaser punches in enough numbers to access the Federal Reserve. The scanner grins--you can see

You can't beat your basic bottle brush pine for both splendor and accessibility

it right there on the screen—and says one number was wrong. Please re-enter.

In the meantime, the line of card-bearing shoppers is growing restless because some of their cards expire at midnight. Children fuss. Carts rattle ominously. Electronic pickpockets eye the crowd for jeans with a nice fit.

And the same scene is playing out in stores across America this holiday season. It actually plays year-round, but is more evident at Christmas because we're all out there in the trenches.

That is why I am proposing a return.

Not a real return, the kind that gets you another plastic gift card that you can spend again in the store where you screwed up the first time. I am typing about getting back together with George (one dollar), Abe (five dollars), and very rarely, Ben (100 dollars—jackpot!).

What a wonderful reunion we would all enjoy. Instead of rolling the dice with disgruntled scanners, people could just reach into their unleaded wallets and purses, bring up handfuls of actual money and hand it over.

Of course, the cashier (irony alert) would have no idea what to do with it. When handed real money, most cashiers extract a marker from their till and swipe it across the bill, just to confirm it's not a credit card.

Having confirmed the marker is still working, the cashier will hand you whatever the till says because making change, like writing in cursive and putting on your wig to go out and run the country, is just oh-so-yesteryear.

See you in line this Christmas, and please keep the kiddies away from your cards.

Testing, Testing

It's 4 a.m. on Christmas Eve. The dog got me up, whining to go out, and now the gift of sleep eludes me.

I contemplate trading her in for a new Christmas puppy, preferably one that is battery operated. Then, on an even naughtier note, I conspire to come up with a Christmas-themed quiz that is sure to stump even the merriest of readers. Ho ho ho!

Call me The Grinch, but it's 4 a.m. and you're sound asleep and I'm being kicked on the couch by a dog that is now dreaming of chasing squirrels. Rather than kicking back, which would just wake her up and make her want to go out again, I get busy as an elf with the "Morning Before Christmas Quiz."

As with quizzes past, it is fraught with vagaries, duplicity, and other words that mean I aim to stump the reader, big time. I hope you are sleeping well, because Naughty Nancy is sharp as a tack and clearly on a mission.

It could be worse. I could have majored in education.

On that happy note, following are 10 words or terms directly related to Christmas. Three definitions are provided for each. Your job is to pick the one closest to the truth. If you fail, you are a Christmas Loser.

Just kidding! Now you see why Santa never left me a key to the teacher's lounge. Answers are provided at the end of the quiz, and in the spirit of Christmas, everyone who participates earns a performance-based, light-hearted, season-friendly title.

Like me, it is non-redeemable. Merry Christmas! And, begin:

Morning Before Christmas Quiz

1. **reindeer**—A. last chance to fill your hunting tag B. how you drive a deer C. deer of tundra and sub-arctic regions

2. **sleigh**—A. what you do to reindeer B. mode of winter transportation C. what I do to my husband in cribbage

3. **Santa Claus**—A. Christmas gift-giver B. Santa's legal defense for home invasion, many counts C. person who won't be visiting me due to cribbage fib

4. **angels**—A. anyone under age 5 in Christmas Pageants B. persons most likely to incur riots during Christmas Pageants C. spiritual beings

5. **bough**—A. front of your boat B. what you deck the halls with C. what angels do at end of Christmas Pageants, in spite of their behavior

6. **stocking**—A. what Elf on a Shelf does B. what Santa fills C. what we do to our shelves when world leaders Tweet about nukes

7. **fir**—A. for, as in, "what fir?" B. what animals wear C. your basic pine

8. **Rudolph**—A. the red-nosed reindeer B. easy target C. what mothers call their Rudys when they're in trouble

9. **bowl full of jelly**—A. Santa's six-pack B. good name for college football game played at Christmas B. that cranberry sauce you can slice

10. **Yule log**—A. what loggers tell their heirs B. what you do when your woods need thinning C. what you light when your house needs atmosphere, or heat

Answers

1-C, 2-B, 3-A, 4-C, 5-B, 6-B, 7-C, 8-A, 9-A, 10-C

100 percent: you're a Wise Man

80 percent: you're a hairy shepherd

60 and under: you are an absolute angel!

Christmas is for Crafters

It all began one starry night, in a little village long ago.

Four kings approached a stable with gifts of frankincense, gold, myrrh, and a tabletop Christmas tree made from circles of white netting stacked on a dowel, accented with glitter and miniature ornaments.

The crafted gift failed to make the cut for the Christmas story, but Mary was hooked. Laying the Babe in the manger, she snipped some wool off a nearby sheep, then knit a pair of Christmas slippers for Joseph.

Flush with her crafting success (they even had pom poms), she gathered some straw and wove a rustic wreath for the house/stable. As the star overhead faded, she was still tying off sackcloth and pine sachets for the visiting shepherds.

Word travels fast in crafting circles. Before you knew it, the marketplace was flooded with quilted donkey blankets, goblet koozies, and everybody's favorite, crocheted camel toilet roll covers in both one hump or two.

Christmas has been for crafters ever since. The problem with crafting is, we all think we can do it. The materials are at hand. We have hands. The only thing that lies between us and prime realty at the Louvre is putting them all together.

That is why I am burning wood this Christmas season.

I burn wood every Christmas. It heats our house year-round. The difference this year is, I am using a wood burner to create lovely pictures on small blocks of pine. Then I chuck the sorry outfits straight into the woodstove.

My story started one sunny afternoon, in a local gift shop a short while ago. I admired a lake scene on a little wooden plaque, created by a local woodburning artist, and had one of those revelations: We have lots of wood scraps! And my brothers' old Boy Scout wood burner! I could create fine art, too!

It was a controlled burn, but just barely. The tool warmed up faster than the artist, from "cool" to "incinerate" before I could warm my coffee. When the smoke finally cleared, I keenly perceived with my artist's eye that I had succeeded in creating charcoal. And it wasn't even good-looking charcoal.

I returned to the gift shop, this time as a humbled customer with lots of dollars in hand, but I just know I can crack the crafting nut. All I need is a little practice, a bigger scrap box, and maybe a Christmas miracle for good measure.

Checkers, Anyone?

If you can believe what the media says or types, hi-tech toys are ruining our children.

This is no big news, which is why you are reading it here. Every generation thinks the next one is doomed, just because the kids don't appreciate the Monkees, bell bottoms (big bells, preferably striped), and Gilligan's Island.

My particular generation, the one that tends to slow down all the rest in supermarket lines and on freeways, the only generation that ever was, is the baby boomers. We were born as a direct result of WWII. Our daddies were very happy to come home to our mommies.

They expressed their joy by populating the earth with many children who were easily entertained. That is because there was so much booming going on, our parents couldn't afford batteries to power enough toys for all their kids.

When Christmas rolled around, all of us baby boomers got basically the same things: dolls, toy trucks, tea sets, sleds, and a few items of clothing our older siblings hadn't already worn. God bless us everyone!

Christmas morning would be a flurry of unwrapping and playing. Then our parents would bundle us up to head outside, resulting in yet another toy tucked under next year's Christmas tree for the newest baby boomer.

It truly was a wonderful life, and it still is, because there isn't a whole lot of traffic in the board game aisle during the Christmas shopping season. That's because everyone who was born after us is fighting over the last Hatchimal.

In case you haven't heard, Hatchimals are this season's Roy Rogers cowboy boots, or Dale Evans boots for girls. They are a hi-tech toy you hatch from an egg, then raise, then fry easy over with a side of sausage or bacon.

Ha! Gotcha', Skipper! (Gilligan's Island reference, youngsters). No, Hatchimals are disturbing little bird-like toys. They hatch from their toy eggs and go through three life phases, all under the loving guidance of a kid that can't hit the laundry basket.

As a sworn watchdog for the public, I went the extra mile and looked up Hatchimals on You Tube. You won't believe what I found, especially if you still have fond memories of Betsy Wetsy, even though she generated lots of laundry.

First of all, you have to hatch your Hatchimal. You do this by picking up your egg, tapping it, twisting it vigorously, and even turning it upside down until the Hatchimal gets "rainbow eyes." You can see them, right through its shell, and then it starts pecking its way out.

If this does not send up a warning flag, then I am not a card-carrying member of the Keith Partridge fan club. Is this how we want our sons to someday initiate their own children's births? Will their wives' "rainbow eyes" be the last lights they'll ever see?

And it only gets worse. Once hatched, the thing sings "Hatchy Birthday." Then your child teaches it to walk, talk and dance through a series of commands including hand clapping, squeezing the toy's belly and tapping it on the head.

The toy responds by rolling around, flapping its wings, making annoying noises and flashing its eyes. When the toy reaches its final stage, which should ideally be end stage, your child can re-program it to start the horrible cycle all over again.

If my father had ever seen one of them under our Christmas tree, he'd have stomped it like a bug. Then he would have sent us all outside, sledding on our new Radio Flyers so there could be even more sensible toys under the tree next Christmas:

- Like Betsy Wetsy, who taught me that if I ever had children, I should severely restrict their fluid intake,

- and the Lionel train set, complete with a missile launch car that my brothers used to shoot the ornaments right off our Christmas tree.

I can still hear the merry tinkle of Mom's Shiny Brite ornaments cascading down on the manger scene below, the one with the Baby Jesus that was slightly chewed by Dad's very first Christmas gift to Mom, a real live Cocker Spaniel puppy named Penny.

Checkers, anyone?

Three Kings Rule

It was music time for the kindergarten class at Sacred Heart elementary school, and like usual, most of them were caught napping.

It's not their fault that music cuts into their rug time. It's almost Christmas, and there's students I haven't even met yet because they score high in sleeping. But that's alright, because music with volunteer guitar strummer Miss Nancy is kind of a lark, and not everyone's a canary.

Just two weeks back we'd had a record house, nearly half the class. The children were on fire, rocking to everything I played while their teacher, Miss Tulppo, kept up a steady chorus of "Crisscross applesauce!" (code for cross your legs and sit down).

Consequently, I had big hopes for this past week, figuring word would get around and I'd score the full roster. But when the clock struck one, prime nap time, just three little boys filed into the library for music, while the rest kept up a steady snore next door.

Miss Tulppo apologized for the slim turnout. I assured her that Three Kings were all we needed for music at Christmas. Then we proceeded to make the most of our monarchy.

There is a short skit called "The Three Kings" that played perfectly for our team. I lined the boys up, assigned parts, and with just a little prompting, watched the magic unfold:

Three great kings on a cold winter's night, found the baby Jesus, guided by the light.

The first one said, "We've come so far." The second one said, "We followed the star."

The third one said, "Great gifts we bring," and together they said, "Great praises we sing!"

OK, so the script wasn't much, but the three royals were pure gold. They spoke loud and clear. They stayed focused. Nobody got poked in the eye, mostly because with a cast of three, we had a lot of room to spread out.

There was no doubt about it—we just had to take this show on the road!

We lined up and processed, skipping just a little, down the hallway to the principal's office, where Mrs. Miron graciously received her wandering minstrel and players. There, the Three Kings proceeded to put on one of the finest shows of the Christmas season.

They shivered in the cold. They all pointed in the right direction, which was just up, but degrees have been known to vary. The second king even dropped his voice a little and added a tremor, an impressive feat when your pipes are just five years old.

The performance was a hit! Mrs. Miron couldn't get too carried away, or she'd have to repent on the pew outside her office that former principal Mrs. Sands dedicated to "My little angels." But she was still smiling wide as we processed out her door and back to the library.

Crisscross applesauce once again, the boys settled down and got back to the serious business of singing. We also put a little added shine on that timeless classic, "Twinkle, Twinkle Little Star," that they would perform at their upcoming school-wide Christmas program.

Who knew Twinkle was the Star of Bethlehem? It was a revelation, and so was the third King who leaped to his feet as soon as the song ended and loudly proclaimed, probably waking several of his classmates next door, "Let's go sing it for the principal!"

We wish you a Merry Christmas.

It's Another Perfect Tree

The tree's branches occur at infrequent and too-few intervals. The longest ones are around its middle. It does have one full spot, where four gnarly little twigs vied for the angel's perch at the top, but nobody won.

Don't ask me how we manage it, just a gift I guess, but once again we've found the perfect Christmas tree. It's grand without being gaudy, and stately, yet not overbearing. Best of all, you can see right through it to the kitchen clock.

Relieving the woods of their most pitiable pine is a hallowed tradition in our home. It may be rooted in the fact we didn't have many ornaments when we first married, and a tree with just eight branches carried the load nicely. Or maybe that first Christmas was extra cold, and we didn't care what we cut down.

I do know that when we blow the dust off our oldest photo album, and reminisce about the diamond- shaped pine slightly listing on our plywood floor, it just inspires us to get back out into the woods and do worse.

I was not raised to cull Christmas trees. My childhood memories are of shuffling through the snow at Gee Lumber on Chicago's South Side (as in, "Gee, who needs lumber in the inner city?") and trying to imagine how those tightly bound trees would look unstrung.

While my three older brothers and I ran around snow-covered lumber piles, pelting each other with pine cones, Mom and Dad figured it out, and always got it right. The tree rode home in the trunk, defrosted in the basement, then was carried aloft with much fanfare into our small apartment.

There it was lovingly decorated, with a timeworn creche our folks bought for their first tree. My contribution was lovingly placing all the animals inside the stable to stay warm, while leaving Baby Jesus adrift out on the rug.

Those are my memories. Our youngsters' memories begin in the summer, when their dad is driving the pickup through our woods and accidentally rolls over a scrubby little pine. It is officially marked for greatness that coming Christmas.

What better attribute could a potential Christmas tree have, than it was a goner anyway? It's still mostly green, has a flat side so it fits nicely against the wall, and has that lovely scent that comes from mashed pine needles.

Sure, it loses them a little early in the holiday season. About a quarter of them fall off while we're hauling it into the house. But it has its day in the sun, and allows us to say in action rather than words: we're really sorry we mowed you down with our pickup truck last summer.

Sometimes we choose imperfect trees for purely sentimental reasons, like the one I hid behind while I tried to threaten a deer to death. It was my first year of hunting, and I had everything I needed except for that vital ingredient called "conviction."

I watched a spikehorn come in, then tracked his progress through my scope for a long time, all the while muttering, "I'm going to shoot you." He ambled so close that all I could see through my scope was a circle of brown fur: "I sure could shoot you now!"

He finally got fed up and walked away. Conviction and meat for our freezer have happened many times since, but pound for pound, I had just as much fun scoping out the buck I didn't shoot.

I obviously didn't need the tree to hide behind anymore, so it was a natural choice that December. After we cut it down, we discovered the stump of another small tree right beside it that could have been harvested for another Christmas long ago. I wondered if those folks were mighty hunters, too.

My brother, Jim, liked to share a heartwarming story with anybody who'd listen about a Christmas tree he'd once cut for us. It was a snowy December, and as he kneeled to saw it at its base, I gave it the tiniest shake, just to admire its form.

As Jim disappeared under a blanket of white, I finally understood why Gee Lumber wrapped its trees.

I think of Jim each year as I shake the snow from another likely candidate. I remember the tree I hid behind, and the little diamond that shone with 35 lights and exactly 12 ornaments on our first Christmas tree in Watton.

And as I watched our five-year-old daughter effortlessly drag this year's pine toward home, leaving a ragged and needle-strewn trail behind her, I knew we had another perfect tree.

14. WHAT'S BUGGING US

Nowhere to Hide

I flipped open the cap on my shampoo, and knew just how Janet Leigh felt when Norman Bates joined her for a shower in *Psycho*. There was an earwig underneath it. And it wasn't finished bathing.

The bug scrambled for a towel. Unlike Janet, who shrieked loudly and emitted large quantities of chocolate syrup to the background music of "REE! REE! REE!", I just ended the little devil under my thumb and got on with it.

That is the difference between Hollywood and the U.P. We are used to being bugged and having nowhere to hide. If Norman had made his move on a Maki in the sauna, she'd have parted his hair with a pickaxe.

For the blessedly uninformed, earwigs look like the love child of a scorpion and a cockroach. They have long antennae, segmented bodies that crunch underfoot, especially when you're barefoot, and nasty looking pincers on their backsides.

According to Orkin, a pest control business that should seriously consider more franchises in the U.P., earwigs are a much-maligned bug. It began back in medieval times, when folks used to rack each other up for entertainment. They believed earwigs burrowed through your ears into your brain.

Of course, modern man knows better. Aliens burrow through your ears into your brain. Earwigs hide in wet spots during the day, including Suave Shampoo & Conditioner, then come out at night to feed exclusively on insects, foliage, and your nerves.

Earwigs are, unfortunately, not the only bugs that blow our collective cool. If you are a berry picker, you should drive a Bloodmobile out to the patch, because this summer's mosquitoes and biting flies are cleaning up on our platelets.

Berry picking is a traditionally relaxing occupation, whereby you wander through the woods or plains with a pail in hand, hitting the dirt whenever vehicles pass so they won't discover your "honey hole." And it still is, except this year the bugs are lying in wait for the lambs-to-the-slaughter.

You arrive at the patch to the soothing sounds of soft wind in the pines, birds chirping, and the occasional cricket. You move into the woods in search of berries that have grown plump in the shade. Then somewhere off in the distance, you detect a high-pitched hum.

It grows louder. More hums join in. Then all of a sudden, you're slapping yourself silly, taking care not to spill your berries while trying to send a swarm of bloodthirsty mosquitoes to their final reward.

That's when you start seeing spots.

They're sand flies. Or black flies, deer flies, horse flies or all four flies, just looking for an opening in your outerwear so they can take a chunk out of your hide. When they're not drawing your blood, they're just hovering, until all you hear in nature is "REE! REE! REE!"

If you flee, they will follow. If you stay, there will be pie.

The answer is clear in the land of the free and home of the fiercely scratching. See you in the berry patch! Hopefully, you won't see me.

A butterfly alights on a lilac bush--because nobody wants to open their book to an earwig

Bees Do It

The wonderful world of beer making is all abuzz, and it has nothing to do with modern inventory.

A new beer-making yeast has been discovered, on the wings of wasps and bees. Considering that for the past 600 years, mankind has had only two yeasts to work with, ale and lager, "bumblebeer" yeast has taken the world by swarm.

The discovery was made, predictably enough, on a college campus. Scientists in a lab at North Carolina State University were studying the biology of food when one of them made a beer run. Scientifically speaking, "he ran tests to find microbes capable of producing beer."

That is the problem with sending scientists out on a beer run. They bring back microbes instead. Luckily for man and womankind, this time they hit the nail on the head, or maybe the wasp between the eyes, and found that pollinators are beer drinkers' best friends.

According to the lab report, two bugs were killed in the making of the scientific discovery. In their defense, one scientist noted, "You have likely killed more bugs on your way to a bar to get beer than we did in the process of making it."

Tests are ongoing to determine the reliability of that claim. In the meantime, the bugs were scientifically smooshed and placed in a petri dish where, just four steps later, they literally became the toast of the college town.

It was beer! And it came from a wasp's wings! And it went well with chips!

Actually, it was sour beer, which some people think is good beer. Bee yeast can produce a range of flavors including a sweet beer that doesn't even have any honey added. According to the National Public Radio reporter who scored the plum assignment, bumblebeer is the bee's knees.

Thanks to a strong work ethic espoused by the bee community, it's timely, too. Craft sour beers can take months or even years to make. Bees get the job done in a few weeks flat. And Italian researchers have a sneaking suspicion that our food and favorite drink source may have been bugged from the start.

According to the Italians, wine is still better than beer, but the very first beer label may have owed its existence to yeast-bearing bugs. They conjecture that a bug hauling a fermenting yeast may have fallen into some wet grain. Soon after, the village was up for grabs.

Some even argue that agriculture began with man's desire to create even more wet grain for the bees to fall into.

While bees everywhere quake in fear at becoming the next main ingredient in barley pop, beer drinkers can thank their lucky stars they found their way home last night. Also, for living in a world where history happily repeats itself in 12-ounce cans or pint size glasses.

Which is more than the poor bugs stuck in our car grills can say.

The Third Plague

It is a little-known fact, mostly because I just made it up, that right after Moses laid down the law, "An accursed insect fleweth into his face and did smite him, right at the hairline."

As long as I'm playing it fast and loose with the Good Book, I might as well add the bug to the Ten Plagues of Egypt, but guess what? It's already number three on the list! The Biblical plague that plagues us still is black flies.

Black flies take center stage this year in my annual salute to bugs that help keep the U.P.'s population in check. Without them, we'd be just another overcrowded metropolitan peninsula with lots of trees and a serious snow problem.

With them, the only heavy traffic we encounter is in the bug repellent aisle.

Black flies go by many names, most of them unsuitable for print, but according to general entomology they are a proud member of the Diptera order. The order also includes mosquitoes. Both bugs bite. If they are real mothers, they draw blood, too.

I mean, "females." Female black flies have an insatiable appetite for blood, like those anemic teens in the *Twilight* series minus the large fan base. Whereas a male will fly a wide circle around mammals to woo a woman, females zero in so they can have more kids.

Even the black flies that don't bite, bite. They fly into our mouths and lodge in our eyes. They land under our hat brims and dangle upside down, making nasty little black fly faces at us.

I just made that up, too, but only because I am far-sighted and can't make out their little fly features.

Black flies first appear as early as mid-March, and are in full force by the end of May. Unfortunately, so is the Memorial Day holiday, when crowds gather in cemeteries across the land to flap their arms, dance in place, and slap themselves silly as black flies swarm their heads in a pre-natal feast.

Unfortunately, there is little we can do to defend ourselves against the tiny foes. Protective clothing is recommended, but PPE is hard to come by these days, and makes you stand out even more when you're dancing in the cemetery because a bug snuck under your face shield.

Chemical warfare is another option, but you've got to bring out the big guns. If your bug spray includes soothing aloe, fragrant oil, or a promise to soften your skin, black flies sporting maternity wear will eat you alive.

You want pesticide on your side, in your face, and especially around your ankles, the kind that features a skull & crossbones on its label and a warning from the surgeon general: "This product kills black flies. If it doesn't kill you first."

Or, you can stay inside during peak periods, defined as basically all of May and June. A second opinion added that black flies are thickest in early morning, the hour after sunset, and just before it rains.

Have a great time in Pure Michigan between times, and don't spare the DEET.

We're the Most Invasive

Q: Which invasive species poses the greatest threat to Pure Michigan?

1. emerald ash borers

2. sea lampreys

3. people

If you chose number three, you win, though we're all basically losers. People do more damage to the earth than any other species, many of which we have already succeeded in wiping out. Also, I'm only picking on Michigan because you never know how the Russians will react.

Ever since Eve said, "C'mon, Ad, it's a McIntosh!", man and womankind have been heck-bent on taking earth down. We don't do it intentionally. To quote a famous rock band, whose name evades me because I'm kind of classic country, we just want to "live and let die."

That's two quotes in one paragraph. Time to get original again.

Each spring, we are bombarded with ads warning us not to spread the threat of invasive species. Topping the list in the U.P. is the emerald ash borer, a shiny little winged beetle that kills our beloved trees.

People cut down entire forests. We do it in an environmentally responsible manner, with permits and everything, but when was the last time you spotted a Wanted sign in the woods featuring a local logger's smiling face?

Our house is made of wood. We burn wood to heat it. I take notes on paper. In the winter, I write my notes on paper with wooden pencils because the ink in my pen seizes up in the cold.

Death to the emerald ash borer!

We also need to be diligent about not introducing invasive species into our fair waters, and believe you me, there are any number of foreigners knocking at the door. Sea lampreys and spiny water fleas are already here, and heads-up: Asian carp could be landing soon.

Invasives compete with and crowd-out native species, and we love our native species. They're delicious! To my personal credit, I've unfortunately taken smaller bites of that apple. If fishing licenses were pro-rated, Pure Michigan would end up owing me money.

Commercial fishing and land mismanagement have helped nudge some of our native species right over the edge and into oblivion. Grayling are history, though we're all hoping recent plantings will someday bear fish, and other native species are under attack, even as I type.

Death to the sea lamprey!

And oh, how we wish it ended there. We gobble up fossil fuels to run our cars (Henry Ford was born here!), drink unleaded water from plastic bottles (uh, so was Rick Snyder), and sometimes leave a lead jig at the bottom of Lake Superior because our knot slipped (my bad).

No invasion is too small or too big, as evidenced in the spread of huge windmills across our fair landscape. The wind isn't even safe from us. That is why action needs to be taken here and now to stop the spread of invasive Michiganders.

In a campaign title lifted straight from my Michigan DNR Fishing Guide (I borrowed a little text, too), you can "Help Stop the Spread" of Michiganders by taking the following precautions this upcoming, highly invasive summer season:

- Remove all Michiganders from your boat before crossing state lines to prevent their spread to your fair state. It already has enough problems of its own, and their wives would eventually miss them. Please release all cans along with them to (re)fund their next fishing venture.

- Do not transport chainsaw-bearing Michiganders into your campgrounds. They cut wood to feed their families and heat their homes, and our campground hosts are reluctant to disarm them. If you encounter one in the woods, do not hug a tree. Their threat of deforestation is real.

Then how would I take my notes in the winter?

15. FOOD FOR AUGHT

Weighing In on Lists

If there is one thing that stops me in my tracks while computing, it's a dead battery.

The second thing is lists, especially ones regarding food.

I love food! I eat it every day. And if you can believe my laptop screen, when it comes to making healthy food choices, Mr. Potato Head (80 calories, 90 with his hat on) has a higher I.Q. than your average American consumer.

Take, for example, *18 Foods You're Eating Wrong*. I thought I'd given up eating wrong when I mastered using utensils. Apparently, there's a lot more to it.

Do you peel your apples and boil your vegetables? As they used to say in my circa-1970s Weight Watchers pamphlet (I really was a master of my utensils), "You are digging your grave with your own fork."

Apple peels contain fiber and antioxidants. They also contain pesticides, which is why you should always rub them vigorously on your shirt or pants leg before eating. Vegetables brim with nutrients. Like a good Finn, they prefer steam over a hot soak.

If you charbroil your meat, you are inviting cancer to your cookout. Cream in your tea? Only if a cardiologist is pouring! And eating pistachios in the shell will save you up to 200 calories, simply because we consumers are too lazy to crack our way through a whole bag.

I could go on and on, but that would displace other vital information that could possibly occur in this book. Instead, I will make all our potato heads spin with: *Six Worst Foods You Can Eat for Dinner*.

Topping the list are frozen dinners, unless they are the venison you just whittled off the carcass still hanging in your garage. Frozen dinners are high in sodium, which is good for preserving deer meat, but people, not so much.

Second on the list is spaghetti with jarred sauce, which in many American households translates to, "Mom cooked tonight!" The meal packs almost as much sugar as an Easter basket, minus the added benefit of your high fiber cellophane grass.

Salad is bad for dinner, because it is hard to stay satisfied after grazing on a bowlful of leaves. Crack a few more nuts and take another lap out to the garage, hatchet in hand, to beef up those greens and help you make it through the night.

For a happy ending to this woeful culinary tale, we turn to *25 Things You Feel Guilty About—For No Reason.* You've gotta' love a list that promotes a second glass of wine because, "that doesn't make you an alcoholic." It just makes you a little lushy.

Activity monitor got you down? Leave it on your dresser! Eat your dessert, cheat on your diet, skip your workout and feel free to cry in public, possibly because your skinny jeans are now cutting you in half.

Take a nap, eat fast food, add more salt, then wash it all down with beer, which supposedly "lowers the risk of developing certain diseases, like diabetes, osteoporosis and Alzheimer's."

Coming soon: *Ten Ways to Avoid Litigation After Listing Bad Advice in Print.*

Beer's Getting Winey

As the clock ticks down to Super Bowl Sunday, game day party hosts are pacing their man caves over what type of beer to serve their guests.

Blue Moon Belgian White? Hoppy Ending Pale Ale? How about a nice, crisp, Lost Coast Brewery Tangerine Wheat?

That is the problem with beer today, minus its tendency to cause loud burps, sometimes in full sentences. It thinks it's wine.

With sincere apologies to wine drinkers everywhere, especially ones with a tendency to comment freely about me on Facebook, wine is kind of hoity-toity. According to the history books, beer came first, remarkably at about the same time man discovered how to get a nice char on his grilled mammoth.

Wine came shortly after, but with a distinct difference. Beer got its start from grain gone wrong. Wine was the product of fruit gone incredibly right, resulting in a pleasing drink that caused an ancient tribe in China to discover the hangover.

We know this to be hard fact, from pottery shards left behind after the party.

Both tasty beverages evoked the same feelings of joy, camaraderie, and severe head pain the following morning. But somewhere along the line, perhaps during the Brewers vs. Vintners Annual Jousting Match, beer fans and wine drinkers parted ways.

There must have been a spill—rider or drink, could be both— followed by a raised eyebrow, a hearty guffaw, and then the place was up for grabs. Wine drinkers took the high road and beer drinkers took the low road, both squealing their cart wheels as they went.

Wine drinkers have enjoyed a certain savoir faire ever since, while beer drinkers have just enjoyed their beer. The facts speak for themselves and are clearly indisputable, unless you have been imbibing, in which case everything is disputable.

Wine is bottled. Beer is canned. Wine is savored. Beer is swilled. Wine ages nicely in cellars. Beer just gets skunky in your garage.

That was then, this is now. It was the title of a popular coming-of-age book teachers assigned bored high schoolers during the last century. It also describes the transformation of the beer industry, thanks to a few insightful brewers who got crafty.

Craft beer is made by a brewery that is small, independent and traditional. It is a specialty beer, usually produced in limited quantities, featuring distinctive and often artistic labels. Nowadays, like the Miller beer ads of yore once proclaimed, craft brews are the "champagne of bottled beer."

People can't get enough of craft beers. Instead of going to a bar and ordering a Bud, they go to a microbrewery and order a flight. It's an assortment of short beers that allows them to test the waters before committing to a full mug.

Beer drinkers are studying labels instead of crushing them behind their belt buckles, and discussing the attributes of IPA. Can swirling and sniffing be far behind?

May your flights be smooth and your landing happy on Super Bowl Monday.

Flying High on Chocolate

A baby is God's opinion that I should never have to stop trick-or-treating.

That is the quote I quoted during the family planning phase of our marriage. If you remember it differently, you are obviously not under the influence of too many junior Kit Kat bars. And you are not welcome in my trick-or-treating car pool, either.

The truth is, someone in this room has a problem with sugar. And for just one night of the year, I am not above exploiting children, first our own and now our grandchildren, to gather the harvest in on Halloween night.

Before we had our own trick-or-treaters, we too shared from our bounty on Halloween. Costumed children knocked on our door. We oohed and aahed. Then they wrestled the candy from my tight fist and went laughing into the night.

This went on for a couple of years, until that magical day one mid-October when the doctor held aloft our firstborn child and said, "Congratulations! It's a girl!"

"It's a trick-or-treater!" I replied, sizing her up for a little clown sleeper. "And not a moment too soon!"

It's not easy trick-or-treating with a newborn, trying to balance a baby and all that candy too, but you can't deny someone her rights just because she doesn't have teeth yet.

Two more trick-or-treaters would join her, securing Mom's role as the Halloween chauffeur who gleefully cackled for her fuel: "How about some more of those little Mr. Goodbars, my pretties? HEE HEE HEE!"

Due to their immature taste buds, they didn't even know that if the candy wasn't chocolate, it didn't count. This ol' witch had no difficulty divesting them of the cream of their crop, and they didn't miss the chocolate bars their dad nabbed, either.

I wouldn't dream of crushing a child's candy dream on Halloween night, but I'm not above pushing my chocolate agenda during the off-season. On a recent shift at the school concession stand, a tiny child with a dollar in her hand marched up to the counter, looked up at me and demanded, "Candy! Skittles!"

"But Skittles aren't chocolate," I patiently corrected her. "How's about a nice Snickers bar, or this bag of M&M's?"

"Candy!" the customer repeated, stomping her foot for emphasis. "Skittles!"

Customers are always right, even when they're wrong. I took her dollar, handed over her Skittles, then bought myself a Hershey bar to restore balance in the universe. And no, I did not use her change. I always bring my own Hershey bar money when I work concessions.

There was a time when I, too, exchanged good money for bad candy. In elementary school I paid three cents each for hot dog-shaped pieces of bubble gum. They were candy-coated, and for added appeal, they turned your saliva blood red.

When you spat on the playground, it looked like you were a vampire. It was a kid thing.

Sooner and sometimes later, people outgrow bubble gum and spitting on the playground. It happened to me when the penny candy store quit carrying hot dog gum. I upped my candy ante to a nickel, bought my first Butterfinger, and haven't spit candy since.

There are whole holidays wrapped around chocolate. Santa delivers it at Christmas. Your boyfriend gives it to you for Valentine's Day, unless you marry him and then the source dries up. The bunny leaves it in your basket at Easter, and best of all, it flows from your neighbor's houses on Halloween.

I still get to drive on Halloween night, but now it's "Gummi" that needs fueling, and it has to be chocolate. Thanks to an early dismissal from school last Halloween, the grandkids made a haul. We hit the streets early and still got home late because some people never grow up.

Three days later I was in the candy bag again because the grandkids were at school, and my daughter warned that if I didn't come up for air, she'd stage an intervention. I laughed it off--we addicts are good at that--but visions of rehab were soon dancing through my head.

I could see it plain as day, a building right out of "Hansel and Gretel" but more of a Craftsman style, in dark chocolate. I'd knock back a few roof shingles and be reaching for the trim when the Wicked Counselor would suddenly grab me, cackling around her dripping wad of hot dog bubble gum--

"Hello, my pretty! You'll be bunking in our Concessions Wing--and all we serve are SKITTLES!"

Mutiny From our Bounty

Our five-year-old granddaughter ran for the phone, because she isn't my husband who doesn't even pick up when I call (and we have caller ID). She listened politely, then asked, "Cucumbers?"

I vaulted over her three-year-old brother, who doesn't do phones either, and snatched it out of her hand. The caller was still prattling on about her excess produce, hinting at a good time for a drop-off, when I cut to the chase.

"We're good on cukes!" I brightly said. "Need some zucc-?"

Abundant apple blossoms in the spring mean you'll be a slave to your canner for fall

Then the line went dead.

The harvest is here, and it's open season on everyone. Our deer hunters' motto of "Let 'em go, let 'em grow" is shared by gardeners across the U.P. who produce more produce than we can possibly use, then struggle to unload--I mean, "share" it--with others.

Family, friends and especially enemies are all fair game for the gardener who has too much of good things. The problem is, even those who struggle to grow enough for a decent salad can only take so much pity produce in.

When my friend and fishing partner, Barry, mentioned his garden production was slightly down this year, I struck like a viper, offering him the pick of the litter from crops that were out of control. Like most of what I fish for, Barry refused to bite.

Even in a bad year, U.P. gardens produce plenty. Our own picker patch survived both an early summer drought and our inability to operate a garden hose, bursting into bloom a little late this year but better than ever.

Green beans that languished in the heat are now battling one another for shoulder space. The cabbages are starting to butt heads, and every time I mow, I take out a few more squash vines that got past or through the garden fence.

This season's biggest surprise came in a small package. We got eight tiny grape tomato plants from friends who started more than they needed, another dominant trait among U.P gardeners. They were so little and cute, we didn't even bother staking them.

If we knew what lie ahead, we'd have caged them and buried the key.

They grew up. They filled out. They toppled over onto the onions, blanketed the carrots and are now putting the squeeze on the peas. And all the while, they keep producing more pretty little yellow flowers that will produce even more grape tomatoes.

There is a blushing basketful on our counter. A big bowlful is going with me to work tomorrow, if there's still room on the table between Gale's cukes and Gina's apples. And I only picked about a quarter of the tomatoes because I don't feel entirely safe from the plants, either.

Having recently run from offers of fresh garden produce with free delivery included, I'm a little hesitant to ask others to help lighten my load. You'll be getting the call instead from my cute little granddaughter, because after all, sharing is caring!

Shame on Turkeys

Shaming is big these days. People get shamed for their bodies, their parenting, their politics and now, their Thanksgiving turkeys.

That's right. Shame on big birds.

It's all because of the millennials, that group of Americans calling the shots just because we baby boomers can no longer find our phones. Or our glasses, keys and TV remotes. But if there is one thing we can remember, it's that Thanksgiving is a major production, and the star of it is Big Bird.

Not the Big Bird from Sesame Street, though he does free range and would probably be quite tasty. No, I mean the traditionally great, big, self-basting, golden-brown reason for the season, the Thanksgiving Turkey!

May it rest in bite size pieces.

According to Bloomberg, a worldwide news source that is much bigger than our hometown weekly newspaper (though we totally smoke them at L'Anse Purple Hornet coverage), "Millenials are disrupting Thanksgiving with their tiny turkeys."

Millenials are trying to eat healthier. They're serving fewer dishes to cut back on waste. They're buying smaller turkeys. Some are even buying a Thanksgiving squab.

First of all, let's take a look at the holiday name. It's Thanksgiving. We're supposed to give thanks. In a nation of fast foodies, we are thankful for the opportunity to finally sit down at a table we don't stick to and eat with real utensils.

There is a time and a place for eating healthier. I have no idea when or where that is, but I am pretty sure it's not Thanksgiving Day, when each and every dish is meant to shine, mainly from its high fat content. We are thankful for giblet gravy and real butter.

Second, there are certain expectations that come with the term, "harvest feast," and they don't include "fewer dishes to cut back on waste." I am not saying we are a wasteful nation. I am saying we are a nation that won't let its guests go home without taking some leftovers with them.

The Pilgrims did not cut corners on the first Thanksgiving spread. It was a bountiful feast of corn and venison and fish and a lot of other stuff that would have really benefitted from giblet gravy and real butter. And you can bet their guests didn't go home empty-handed, either.

If there is one point that we can all agree on, it's that smaller turkeys are not an entirely bad idea. Millenials abhor big turkeys because they know it's not natural for birds to grow that large unless they live on Sesame Street. Hence, they must be unhealthy for you.

Baby boomers don't like big turkeys because it hurts our backs to lift them, and they never fully defrost, no matter how many days we leave them out on the counter. Hence, we just cook 'em with the bag of giblets still inside.

And if you are still wondering about that squab, it is a baby pigeon. Eating that on Thanksgiving Day is just plain coo coo.

16. FAMILY MATTERS

Speaking of Dad

My two-year-old grandson was babbling about something the other day when I looked him square in the eye and said, "Ya' talk like a crazy man."

He didn't miss a beat, but I stopped dead in my tracks, because I never say that, and hadn't even heard it in years. It was a favorite saying of my dad's. He's been gone since 2000, and while I'm not actively channeling him, I'm apparently tuned in.

Dad was full of 'em, and full of it, too. Born and raised on Chicago's South Side, he worked in the stockyards, fought in WWII, married his childhood sweetheart and raised four kids on a food broker's wages, not far from where he'd started.

And oh, the wisdom he gained along the way. He didn't share much of that with us—wisdom can't compete with your friends waiting to play kick-the-can in the alley—but we sure got a healthy helping of fun, like the Women's Christian Temperance Union's theme song that Dad so loved to sing:

We're a-comin', we're a-comin', with a torch in our hand,
On the right side of tem'prance we'll now take our stand
Oink toink toink, oink toink toink, WCTU.

I cannot attest to the validity of the lyrics, especially the "oink toink toink." I tried Googling it, but Google never met my dad, who crooned the song with utter conviction and sometimes with a beer in hand. He'd have us kids in stitches by the end. And that is just the start.

Whenever we were ill, and with four kids there was always someone convalescing on the couch, Mom was our Florence Nightingale. Dad was just a nightingale, with a sum total of two diagnoses to pick from. You either had the Skreebs, Groobers and Worshesnicks or the Chinese Blue Jeans.

If neither of those options made you feel any better, Dad still had an ace up his sleeve to offer comfort in your time of need: "'T'ain't the cough that carries you off, it's the coffin they carry you off in." And if they carried you off, the cause was always "Shortness of breath."

When we were feeling better, and feeling our oats as well, he'd rein us in by raising his hands, curling them into not-terribly-threatening fists and once again giving you your pick: his right, "instant death," or left, "permanent disability."

I usually dove between them both for a bear hug. Dad couldn't even pull off a threat with the family dog, a cocky little West Highland Terrier who absolutely adored him. Rags' rule book was pretty thin, but she was strictly forbidden from eating her dog biscuits on the dining room rug.

Rags would pick a biscuit out of her bowl, trot into the dining room, and look expectantly up at Dad. He'd point at her and bellow, "Who do you think you are?" Then she'd turn tail and run under the dining room table, happily crunch her treat, and go back to her bowl and Dad for more.

The grandkids' rule book was even thinner. He'd cuddle with them on the couch, and sneak them cookies and slabs of buttered coffee cake. Or he'd call them into the kitchen for slices of bread, spread thickly with cream cheese and dotted with sliced olives

Then he'd lean in like a fellow conspirator and say, "Now, that's livin'!"

Now I share his sayings and songs for him, and for me, and for my own small herd of grandchildren who will someday look down upon a babbling great-grandchild and say, "Ya' talk like a crazy man."

And wonder where the heck that came from.

Working, With Children

Before you invite this reporter into your home or business for an interview, or to your club's next banquet to photograph an award presentation, there's something you should probably know first.

I don't always work alone.

On any given assignment, I may have one and as many as three assistants by my side. They are the reason I quit working at the newspaper nine years ago, and they're part of the reason I recently returned.

Ideally, I had hoped to wait until our heirs were all in school before I came back to work. But when the opportunity recently arose to start reporting again part time, we settled for two out of three. Since then,

Many hands lighten up my work

and especially when school is out, my assignments have often been covered by four.

Our first family assignment opened my eyes to some of the changes three children can bring. We went out one evening to take photos of a boys' basketball game. After seating my four-year-old, six-year-old and eight-year-old on the bleachers at mid-court, I set up behind a hoop and started shooting.

It felt wonderful to be back in the game! The roar of the crowd, the squeak of players' sneakers as they ran up and down the court--nothing had changed, until another, vaguely familiar sound rose above the rest: Dimme a tiss.

Huh?

"Dimme a tiss! DIMME A TISS!"

Abandoning my post, I raced over to the irate little blonde bouncing on her seat and gave my youngest her kiss. Granted, I missed some action under the hoop, but I prevented even more on the bleachers, successfully executing my first play in the ongoing game of working with children.

Gwen let me go under the condition I'd return often. At halftime she requested a trip to the washroom. Sam, age 6, hopped in unspoken agreement, so we went to find facilities that, in my past life, I'd never had to bother locating.

Back again, Katy, age 8, informed me she was starving. Sam agreed to that too, so I bought my first candy bar from the concession booth. Then I walked my team back to the bleachers, kissed Gwen, and picked up my camera again.

There are few assignments in Baraga County that aren't family-friendly. Thanks to some help where you'd never expect it, there are plenty of other gigs that go well with kids.

Who knew there were toys at the Baraga County Equalization office? Nobody at the DNR office in Baraga ever broke out the balloons, coloring books and stickers until I brought my assistant along. Then they loaded the kid for bear.

Gwen has eaten 100th birthday cake with residents at the Skilled Nursing Unit, romped with a security guard's English Bulldog and, along with her siblings, attended her first L'Anse High School Senior Girls Tea. And they even got served.

Sometimes there are lessons to be learned in assignments we share. My son dropped exactly one dime at a local turkey shoot's infamous ten-cent raffle before concluding, "I ain't buying them tickets. You pay ten cents and you don't win nothin'."

The girls and I littered the floor with losing tickets, but I was glad at least one of us saw the light.

When we witnessed a harmless but graphic rollover at the county fair mud drag, it provided Mom a golden opportunity to preach: "Never, EVER drive like him!" And when Mom was out of range one night, it provided the kids with an opportunity to do some preaching, too.

I was covering an award presentation, and briefly left my trio on a bench at the back of the Knights of Columbus Hall with a request to keep the peace. As I prepared to snap a photo up front, the littlest started an argument with the next sibling up the line.

Pretty soon all three were at it, and I was too far away to intervene. A blessedly short time later, the man accepted his award to the flash of a camera and a loudly bellowed, "SAMMY, MOM SAID TO BE QUIET!"

If you're going to fail, it's good to do it where a Christian attitude prevails.

We once covered a new car wash opening, a Christmas raffle and a tribal fish hatchery planting in Keweenaw Bay, all in one long evening after school. Between times we ate at a diner, stuffed raffle boxes and toured town to see the Christmas lights.

It's a busier career than the one I remember, but it's working, with children.

Focus on Photography

There is something horribly wrong with a society that requires its young to become certified in Hunter Safety before handling a gun, yet will put a fully loaded camera into a child's hands at a wedding and say, "Get a shot of Daddy doing the Chicken Dance!"

If I were president, first I would look for another job. Second, I would pass a bill while Congress was sleeping that would require people with cameras to become licensed before they shoot.

Cameras, like weapons of mass destruction only much more insidious because high school yearbooks are forever, have come a long way. The earliest models were big and unwieldy and often required the use of explosives, much like your modern-day rock concerts.

It took a long time for early cameras to capture an image. That is why our ancestors looked either stiff or blurry but always cranky in photos from yesteryear. They had been holding their pose for several days, and desperately needed to visit the outhouse.

People developed a healthy fear of photography, and that was good, but as time marched on cameras became smaller, pastel-colored and mainstream. The 1960s produced a camera that spat prints right into your hands, where they'd develop right before your eyes.

Over fifty years later, the Polaroid Swinger's advertising jingle still haunts my memory, a lot like my high school senior picture.

Swing it up, it says "Yes!"
Take the shot, count it down, zip it off!

Cameras are clearly the devil's own invention, and make adults quake in fear while toeing the line at the DMV. However, children are another story altogether. They embrace the voodoo that is modern photography. They want to shoot back.

Nowadays, children have their first photo taken before they even leave the hospital. They invite their pediatrician to lean into their bassinet, then use their cell phone to snap a shot before heading home, sharing it along the way with friends they made in the nursery.

Just kidding! Babies have their first photo taken by mature adults with a high tolerance for capturing squalling, red-faced images. And did you know that Barry Manilow of "Copacabana" fame sang the Polaroid Swinger jingle?

Segueing neatly back to the present, many children get their start in photography at wedding receptions. Tables are often set with a disposable camera or two, so guests may capture candid shots to complement the professional photographer's images.

The problem with that is, children.

Children are gifts from God above, but it can be hard to prove at wedding receptions. They become restless and bored. They see a toy on the table. They find its shutter button. Before you can say "Gimme that!", they are blinding other guests with a volley of camera flashes aimed up their noses.

Then they get bored with that, too, and commandeer the dance floor.

After the honeymoon and an expensive trip to the photo shop, the couple will boast a collection of shots of their guests' noses, knees, and the occasional full facial of their wedding photographer mouthing a very bad word.

By the time they reach their teens, kids have perfected taking photos of one another, preferably behaving badly. It is the new take on keeping a secret diary, only worse, because pictures speak louder than words. It is hard to say "I didn't mean it" when you are pictured doing it.

While they are quick on the draw, teens often forget to cover their tracks. Their willingness to share their misadventures insures that so long as your budding photographers live under your roof, their chore list is non-negotiable.

Luckily for the kids, shots from this past Christmas bear ample evidence of adults behaving badly, too. Like the man engaged in a Nerf gun shootout with his grown son, and the woman eyeing her new fuzzy slippers with a face that only Jane Goodall could love.

There oughta' be a law.

Family Banking Doesn't Pay

Back when "online" was what you did with wet laundry, I didn't have to tug at my neckline and wink like a temptress to get people to throw money at me. All I had to do was announce, "I'm headed for town--anyone got any banking?"

Before you could say, "What's in your eye, Mom?", it would be raining money in Watton. When the storm was over, I'd be left holding three paychecks, a rebate for a case of oil and a $1.39 refund for overpayment on car insurance (we dropped our antenna coverage).

There would also be a $20 bill someone finally shook out of their Christmas stocking, and an old birthday check that was keeping both an aunt and her bookwork unbalanced. As an afterthought, someone would hand me the spare change jug because it was bending the bookshelf.

It is a mystery to me how somebody who failed "Introduction to Felt Boards" wound up as the family banker. I guess it all began back in my childhood, when my parents say I would stash all my money in my savings account and borrow from them instead.

Then I grew up, took all my money out, and brought it up north to Baraga County. There, my huge influx of wealth greatly endeared me to that irascible banker, Mr. Drysdale, and his zany sidekick, Miss Ja...

My bad! That's the Beverly Hillbillies! When I deposited my money in the local bank, the building didn't even burp. But I did quit my borrowing ways, and finally began living within my means. Then I got engaged to be married, and the living got meaner.

My betrothed and I pooled our resources to build our home before we wed. By pooled, I mean we spent all his money first. By the time we had our basement built and our four walls up, his savings balance officially registered "moths."

We kept the debt collector from our new door by finally swiping the cobwebs off my savings passbook. That put a lid on our castle, and left me in permanent possession of the ultimate trump card: "I put a roof over your head!"

Not that I would ever dream of saying it.

Because they couldn't pedal to the bank, our children usually left their banking up to Mom. This would not be a bad idea if they all just dumped their money into savings and borrowed from me, but they'd heard that "roof" line one too many times, and it cost me dearly.

"Put this check in savings, this one in checking, and bring home the rest, small bills."

"Put half of this $20 in my savings, please, and bring home two fives. But cash this old check first."

"This change can go in the vacation fund, but warn the teller, I think I dropped a screw in there."

The dog would stand sentry as I loaded the week's fortunes into the car, then she'd hop aboard because tellers also handed out treats. As I made my getaway, a teenage waitress could be seen coughing in my exhaust, waving a handful of singles and hollering, "I NEED BIGGER BILLS!"

No problem. I'd be heading back to town for more banking the next day.

The tellers would all be busy when I entered, but if I could make eye contact, the newest one would crack and call me to the counter. As she hauled my coffee can over to the counting machine, I'd busy myself with all the checks my family failed to sign. Remarkably, we shared the same handwriting.

I'd be signing the last few with a flourish when the teller would finally return, brandishing a receipt for the change. She'd also present me with the wood screw, two sea shells from our Florida vacation and a holy medal that failed to make the cut as a quarter.

I'd carefully repeat my instructions as I slid money, checks and rebates under her window. Then I begged a dog treat for my escort, stuffed the envelope of money into my purse and pocketed the oil rebate and $1.39.

Because even family bankers deserve a dividend or two.

Tot Translator

I was driving through town, minding everyone's business but my own (Hmm, they finally got that roof done. Frostie Freeze again? Someone's got a problem with Mint Chocolate Chip!), when the radio interrupted my regular programming with an important message.

"Now you can enroll children as young as two years old in a foreign language class."

"Fer cryin' out loud!" I exclaimed to my dashboard, which is actually my best listener. "Kids already talk a foreign language! How 'bout enrolling adults in a class so we can understand 'em?

I apologize for my English. I chose to study high school German instead. I'd mess with that language, too, but 400 miles is not too far for my German 101 teacher, Sister Clement, to hunt me down and hold me accountable.

Children speak a language all their own. When they tire of their parents' pitiful efforts at translating every word they say, they finally give in and begin to talk like us. Until then, what they're saying is anybody's guess.

Babies understand themselves perfectly, but we forgot their language long ago. They are small but mighty beings, laughing on the inside as full-grown adults lean over them, grin like a fool and ask, "Wanna' baba before sleepoo time?"

They find this absolutely hilarious, but can't laugh out loud because their mouths are plugged with a baba. Instead, they have to wait for us adults to enter the next stage of language development, which is Tot Translation. It's a skill you learn as they grow.

Case in point: granddaughter Tullia, age two. When Tullia says "meese," my daughter says, "thank you." When she requests "appleshoes," my daughter serves her applesauce. And when she smiles at "Bah-tah," Grandpa gives her anything her little heart desires.

At a mature age three, grandson Dawson has a broader range, but puts a different spin on his words. Currently going through a pirate phase, he struts around the house, squinting through a toilet paper roll and growling, "Shimmy timmers" (shiver me timbers).

On a recent errand with my daughter and both grandchildren, we interpreted for each other as the kids carried on a conversation in their car seats. Just to show we cared, we repeated every sentence they said, adding the mandatory question mark at the end.

"You want to play with Maddy when she gets home from school?" (Tullia nods).

"And you want to ride your tractor around the yard, shimmy timmers?" (pirate smiles).

When children and adults finally get into sync with language, there are still some major bumps in the road. Children say it like it is, and from where they're standing, about waist high, the view is a little bit skewed.

We were pulling up to church one morning many years ago when our son, Sam, age four, jumped as high as his car seat would allow and hollered, "Mom! Don't brum on God!"

By "brum" he meant "drive," and by "God" he meant "Fr. Francis Dobrzenski," who was taking advantage of the warm sunshine by greeting parishioners on the church steps. For the record, I have never brummed on a clergyman. And Fr. Fran was delighted with his promotion.

Soon enough we all grow up, and the tables are turned, because now our children and grandchildren have to repeat every word they say to us. They just have to say it a little louder the second time around.

NEW Grandmothers Rock & Roll

In a recent *AARP Bulletin*, which I am obviously receiving prematurely, there is a rather disturbing article about "The NEW Grandmothers."

The article features a photo of actress Jane Seymour with two little grandchildren. One is delicately placing a plastic flower on Jane's head. The other is beaming up at her from her lap.

Did I mention Jane is dressed all in white?

The children are roughly the ages of two of my grandchildren, but are certainly not acting it. Mine adorn me with real flowers, failing to shake the dirt off first. They beam up at me, too, but it's from atop my belly where they gleefully like to pounce whenever I stretch out on the floor to straighten my back. They call the game, "Gummi Down!"

I am not saying my grandchildren are the devil's own. I am saying you would not want to see me in *AARP Bulletin* with a bent back and dirt dripping into my eyes. But I am still the very picture of the NEW grandmother.

Except for the part where, "Today's grandma is more likely to practice yoga than play canasta."

This Gummi doesn't do yoga. I tried, but I drink way too much coffee to keep up with the crowd. I mean, "down" with the crowd. I prefer to get my yoga done in five minutes flat: mountain--inhale--forward fold--lunge--left leg--etc.--STOP THE CLOCK! Then I run to use the bathroom.

Instead, the grandkids and I do road work with the stroller, stopping only to pick flowers, wave at passing pickups and moo at cows. The problem is trying to keep Gummi's heart rate up. Do you have any idea how many flowers, pickups and cows there are in farm country?

Sometimes we do vigorous floor exercises together. I do several repetitions of assorted kicks and stretches. The three-year-old drops down to the floor to join in the fun, lifts her tiny foot, and kicks me right in the head.

Then we laugh and laugh and, as long as we're down there, check under the couch for Barbie's clothes. Barbie has a bad habit of going au naturel. Ken does, too, but only because his pants are so tight, he can't bend to catch a ride in the Barbie Mobile.

My mom never played canasta, but she didn't roll around on the floor with our kids either, because old grandmothers had something NEW grandmothers lack: their dignity.

My mom raised her eyebrows, said stuff like "Oh dear," and kicked naked Barbies under the couch to be with their clothes. Naked Kens, too, different couch.

And I loved Mom for it, and our kids did too, but according to the *Bulletin*, that is not how NEW grandmothers swing. Instead, "We want to share things with our grandkids, have discussions."

Have you ever tried to engage an 18-month-old in a serious discussion? Ours either shakes his head "no" or says "da" when we're in agreement. I think that's Swedish. If we can teach him just one word in English, he'll officially be bilingual. Then I'll understand at least half of our discussions.

The newest model, a five-month-old, coos and chirps and hollers, which is all pretty average yet still outstanding because she is, after all, my grandchild. The oldest has a pretty full vocabulary for just three and a half years of taking it all in, and she's not afraid to use it to straighten out her Gummi.

"I have to go bathroom."

"We're in the woods, sweetie. But you can go in the woods."

"No."

"People go bathroom in the woods."

"No."

"Gummi has even gone bathroom in the woods!"

"I don't wanna' see that."

That was the end of that discussion, and yes, she made it home. So did her Gummi, because as *AARP Bulletin* so astutely reports: "Their engagement with their grandchildren is akin to the way kids used to describe the fun they'd have with a really cool aunt."

I don't know how a really cool aunt behaves, but I think I'm closing in on the look. During a visit a few weeks back, the above mentioned was playing with her scented markers. She uncapped and made me smell each one. They all smelled like grapes gone bad. I thought nothing more about it.

On my way home, I made several stops in town. Later that evening, I glanced in the bathroom mirror. The tip of my nose was several shades of purple, and my hair was askew from several rounds of Gummi Down. I looked like the Cowardly Lion in the Wizard of Oz, right after he'd met the Wicked Witch.

It's a NEW Grandmother thing.

No Escaping Sunday School

Life isn't easy when you're a senior citizen and still in Sunday School.

When everyone runs upstairs into the church, you're the one that gets caught. When everyone is making cardboard sandals, you have to drive to the store for bigger boxes. And you never, ever get confirmed and graduate out.

This is not the way it was supposed to be. I was raised a Catholic, and Catholics don't practice Sunday School. We go to catechism, preferably during school hours to get out of school. But God's favorite words are "Ha ha ha," uttered every time mere mortals try to plan.

Like many years ago, when the doctor delivered our firstborn into the world and announced, "You have a little girl! And she's a Protestant!"

Just joshing. A professional physician would never divulge the denomination of a patient without first securing formal consent. But a proud mother will freely put into print that we were delivered that day of a beautiful baby girl. Lutheran, Missouri Synod to be exact.

My husband's gene would prove dominant in all three heirs. Before you could say, "Where are all the statues of saints?", I was parked in a pew at Trinity Lutheran, re-learning the mass/service said by the priest/pastor while listening to readings from the Bible/Bible.

Same God, different location. After a while, I quit reaching for the holy water when I entered the church, and quit genuflecting (quick kneel) after causing the third pile-up outside our pew. I learned to say "the quick and the dead" instead of "the living and the dead." It's the little things that count.

And the littlest things, our own three Lutherans, counted the most. They flourished in the church, kicking the pew in front of them and folding their bulletins into paper airplanes, just like proper little Catholics would do, too. By the end of the service, they were lucky they were still quick/living.

When our oldest turned four, she went off to Sunday School, with Pastor Allen playing guitar. He also offered to teach it to adults, and I signed right up. If I'd have listened more closely, I'd have heard the faint "Ha ha ha" issuing from above.

Pastor Allen left us way too soon. Before he passed, he told me he was glad that I could play for the kids. God has had me by the guitar strings ever since.

And I'm in fine company, because He's got Debbie by her ability to herd tiny boys into a classroom and mesmerize them with a story about a guy and his boatload of animals. Carole is being held back due to inspiring faith and boundless enthusiasm.

When she leads Sunday School, the journey is always fun. The day we sang a story about Jesus the Fisher of men, Carole snuck a bag of gummy worms into church and flung them to the children, mid-chorus! She's, like, a Lutheran saint.

Viola is much more mature than us, but is called back to Sunday School every Easter and Christmas to play the organ for songs just too majestic for me to strum. When Viola plays, the children naturally toe the mark. Unless Carole brings her bag of worms to church.

The only problem with being a Sunday Schooler in perpetuity is the mixed blessing of watching the kids grow up. One week they're shyly peeking at you from behind their mother, arms tightly wrapped around her legs so she won't leave them behind.

The next, they're towering over their folks, smiling for photos at their confirmation.

In between, they're batting each other over the heads with their shepherd's staffs at Christmas pageants, begging for another chorus of "Pharoah Pharoah" (sung to the tune of "Louie Louie"—forgive me,

Lord) during Sunday School devotion, and learning how to fold their hands to pray.

When they're tiny, they sneak toys into the pew to make church more interesting. When they're big, they jump up to slap the banner hanging from the church balcony. That's when you know they're ripe for confirming.

Some return to help out, or even teach a class of their own. Eventually they all go off to college or to work. But someday, and that day is forever getting closer, they'll come back to Sunday School again, hobbled by a little someone whose arms are tightly wrapped around their legs.

Congratulations, confirmands. Any of you ever consider learning to play the guitar?

17. OLDER, NO WISER

Getting Gamey

As another Women's Slow Pitch Softball season approaches, we more mature members of the league need to ask ourselves: Do I still "get game," or am I just getting gamey?

The question first occurred to me at the tender age of 42. That's because it was written in big, black letters on the cast I earned after a sloppy slide into third base.

"S---!" I said, as I heard a crack that was not the bat.

The umpire called me safe because he was too far away to hear my foul language. Then as I rolled around in the dust, gripping my ankle and grieving the loss of my youth and bone density, the third baseman tapped my butt with her mitt and looked expectantly at the ump.

"Now yer' out!"

After the initial indignity, I was fitted with a pair of crutches and a Fiberglas support sock that pegged me as a slow-moving billboard. Everyone wanted to leave their mark on my Colonial White cast, and I was in no condition to outrun them.

Family, friends and amateur artists enjoyed eight weeks of free advertising on my right leg. It was illustrated with hearts, signatures and a Nike swoosh, but the message it broadcast loudest seemed to be, "Too old to play ball."

I heard even more of it on the streets. I couldn't move fast enough to catch the culprits, but you know who you are, Harry and Ron! Someday you'll be too old for Women's Slow Pitch Softball, too.

A new Women's Slow Pitch season is just getting underway, open to ages 13 and up, with the "up" part left to the discretion of the players. For the sake of my fellow mature athletes, I have come up with a test to determine if you really are still in the game.

Please check the following answers that hit close to home, or just tally them on your cast if you have already been sliding this season. Do your own work, preceding each of the following with, "I am too old for Women's Slow Pitch Softball if..."

1. My favorite athletic footwear is by Dr. Scholls.

2. I have to convince five of my peers to play, too, so we can ride the senior shuttle to our games.

3. The bat feels awfully light in my hands, and then I realize I'm about to swing with my cane.

4. My fans holler, "Go, Grandma!"

5. And their children join in.

6. I win arguments with the ump because I used to babysit him.

7. Batters sometimes confuse my varicose veins with the baseline, and run right up my leg.

8. I lose track of pop-ups between the lenses of my trifocals.

9. Drug screenings are done to make sure I remembered to take them, and

10. The kids write my name on my glove in big letters, so I bring the right one home after the game.

If your scorepad looks like a chicken with dirty feet just danced across it, don't despair. As long as you still enjoy the game, maintain your sense of humor and heal relatively well, you have plenty of years ahead to enjoy playing Women's Slow Pitch Softball.

As for the rest of you, the younger players we'll be squinting at, stumbling after and crumpling at the feet of this coming season, I have just three words of advice: Respect your elders!

Gripers Go Pro

We were driving with our niece Amanda last weekend, basking in the panorama of the Northwoods in their full fall color, when I interrupted with an important message from the backseat.

"Our friend Dennis got a free bag of potatoes from Walmart!"

That is the thing about panoramic afternoons. They allow the mind time to wander, then settle on fond memories of days gone by. It is also the thing about being ever so slightly mossy in America. You have the time and the wherewithal to get your potatoes free from Walmart.

Allow me to explain. "Wherewithal" is an archaic term defined as "money or other resources needed for a particular purpose." And we archaic Americans are swimmin' in the wherewithal.

Our children are grown. Our careers are winding down. We are closing in on covering the principal on our college loans. The world is our oyster!

And are we tipping our heads back, tilting our shells and inviting good fortune to slide down our gullets? I think not! Have you checked the price of oysters lately? We are talking two trips to the thrift store on $5 A Bag Day, and that's just for an appetizer.

That is the other thing about being mature. You tend to watch your pennies. After a lifetime of enduring accidental overcharges, getting shortchanged and having our vehicles recalled ("The good news is, you've got a brand-new air bag!"), we are gunning for bear.

We are the younger generation's worst nightmare, especially if they are standing behind us in checkout. We dig in our purses for coupons that have expired. We check our receipts. We write checks to pay for our purchases, then balance our checkbooks while we're still stooping in line!

I think I just loosed a bubble of mirth. Yeah, we do that in checkout lines, too. But before you run away with your cart to self-checkout, which actually requires extra personnel when we wander there before you, consider the following: we can work together.

Not in the same room of course, because quite frankly, your music is obnoxious. We can't understand the lyrics and it makes our ears throb, especially when we have fresh batteries. No, my niece put it in a nutshell when she exclaimed, "You could work for us!"

You see, Dennis got his potatoes for free because he fought for them. He'd gotten a couple rotten potatoes in his last sack from Walmart. Unlike a newer model, who would just throw them away and get on with it, Dennis is a classic, and actually phoned the store to see that justice was done.

The person who answered somehow got him a free bag of potatoes. I think he got some money back too, or maybe it was two bags of potatoes, but my point is, Dennis cleaned up. And a couple months later, we did, too, when an extended full warranty somehow didn't cover a car repair.

I called corporate, and referencing the car company's popular ad campaign, reported that "I am not feeling the love." I said a lot of other stuff, too, because I had the time and I certainly had the inclination, and a week later I received a full refund for the fix.

It was a revelation. I'd have never done that when I was younger, mostly because I couldn't afford an extended full warranty.

But I and my generation can afford to work for you, because we will obviously work for new potatoes and the occasional check. As Amanda noted, we can pursue justice, mostly on the phone because gas costs good money you know.

We'll call about your rotten potatoes, your cold pizza deliveries and your failing grade in high school English Lit. And if they won't help us, we'll call their mothers. Just call us anytime, as long as it's before 4 p.m. when we close up shop for dinner.

Lifetime Loser

I was struggling to plug in my laptop on the wrong side this morning, when I gave it a half spin and concluded I am losing it.

I promptly forgot all about it, until I realized my reading glasses were absent from my nose. After three laps around the house to find a pair of cheaters that weren't my husband's, I put my glasses to good use, hunting down my coffee cup.

If you are my age in America, you are losing it, too. You are losing your socks, your phone, and your car keys. You endlessly circle the house like a wagon that's lost its train, and your worst fear isn't that you'll have to buy new. It's that you're losing your marbles.

Although I have no medical training, I am confident in typing that you are gravely mistaken. You left your marbles on the playground over 50 years ago! Also, it is perfectly normal to be losing things at our age, because let's face it, we've been losing it since we were born.

Think back. Yes, the car keys are in the cup holder. Good job. Now think back even farther, to a time you remember as if it were yesterday, although yesterday is already kind of a blur. You were a kid. You were losin' it all the time.

First you lost your pacifier. Then your bottle disappeared, followed by a baby shoe. Shortly after, it was your baseball mitt, then a book report, and on into high school when you lost your bedroom floor under a layer of teenage detritus and one baby shoe.

Along the way, you never thought to question your sanity. You were way too cool to care.

Children do crazy stuff all the time. I have personally witnessed, after finding my glasses of course, a young child put a dishtowel over his head and say, "Watch what I can do!", then walk right into a wall. The next day, he did it all over again.

Children roll off couches and cartwheel into coffee tables, and never look over their shoulders to check for witnesses. They're too busy coming up with the next great idea to even care. And even though we are old at heart, I think we should be a little more like them.

First, put down the dishtowel. We're done growing new teeth. Nobody has to take a hit for this team unless they've already met their deductible. Like kids, we just have to own our wild and crazy and sometimes unexplainable actions.

Can't find your socks? Go without. I've seen it in magazines, and the people weren't even boating. Went down into the basement, and can't remember what you were supposed to bring back up? Grab the coffee cup you left on the dryer, check the freezer for the TV remote, and call it good.

If you can find your car keys, take a quick run to the store for the canning lids you finally remembered needing from the basement, just because you're wild and carefree and love to shop. Besides, it's Senior Wednesday, and you get 15 percent off all purchases!

Unless it's Thursday.

Becoming slightly mossy can be a sweet deal with just the right cake and a side of coffee

Do You Wah Diddy?

I have a problem with AM radio. My problem is, I discovered it.

Well, I didn't actually discover it. I just turned it on, and now I can't tune it out, because my mind is stuck in the groove and keeps replaying songs from the sixties that only a baby boomer could love, because of lyrics like:

Every sha-la-la-la, every wo-o-wo-o, still shines,
Every shing-a-ling-a-ling, that they're startin' to sing's, so fine.

It all started back in the early 1900s, when Italian inventor Guglielmo Marconi sent a radio transmission across the Atlantic Ocean. The complete text of that transmission was the letter "s," and won the Grammy that year for Excellence in Early Rap.

No, it didn't. I was just conducting a quality control test of the Federal Broadcast System, which apparently doesn't read. Marconi's transmission led to farther-ranging and considerably more interesting broadcasts, which leads us right back to the source of my troubles, which is AM radio.

My troubles began just two months ago. I was proudly driving our new, gently-used car home from the dealership when I turned on the radio and was rewarded with a blast from the past:

Hello Muddah, hello Faddah, here I am at, Camp Grenada
Camp is very, entertaining, and they say we'll have some fun if it stops raining.

A sensible person would have pulled over and gotten ill. I punched up another of the former owner's favorite AM stations, then another and another until finally Karen Carpenter's voice got so static, it sounded like your modern music.

So I turned it off, and that's where it should have ended, right near the Michigan/Wisconsin border where AM pretty much dies out, but it didn't because:

He's got, high hopes, he's got, high hopes
He's got, high apple pie, in the sky hopes!

And I keep going back for more, especially when the weather is dodgy and signals from the past can catch a ride on precipitation. Instead of tuning into my former favorite radio show, National Public

Radio's highly respectable "All Things Considered," I settle in for a steady diet of goofy, nostalgic static.

My friend and editor, Barry Drue, also enjoys "All Things Considered." We'd both tune in on our rides to work, then enjoy rehashing the stories we'd heard. Now when Barry talks, I just smile and nod politely while listening instead to the silly tunes still running rampant through my mind:

Who put the bomp in the bomp bah bomp bah bomp
Who put the ram in the rama lama ding dong

I finally confessed to my transgression this past weekend, and strangely, Barry didn't seem surprised. Then he said he'd just heard a report on "All Things Considered" about Roger Miller, a composer who cranked out songs any AM station would be proud to play, including "Ya' Can't Roller Skate in a Buffalo Herd."

Barry even sang a few bars for me, because I hadn't heard that one yet, and he admitted he listens to AM, too, but only when they're broadcasting sports.

Like roller skating! In a buffalo herd! Rama lama ding dong.

The Future is Calling

I have a problem with calling my kids. They always answer their phones.

"Hi Mom. What noise? Oh, that's the wind. I'm snowboarding on *Get a Will Hill*. Big jump coming up—I'll call ya' back later."

"Yo' Mama. I'm driving on the interstate. No, that siren wasn't for me. Mom? Mom! Did you hang up on me again?"

It's not that I don't want to know what our kids are up to. I just don't want to put their lives in peril while I'm filling them in on the daily snowfall report for Watton and what I'm reheating for dinner.

Times were when civilized folk curled up with a cup of coffee to talk on the phone. You'd carve a few minutes out of your day, dial a friend and have a pleasant chat. It was the era of no-fault phoning.

Then phone cords got a little longer, so you wouldn't be tied down while talking. You could reach the dishpan while visiting. You could also drop the phone into it, giving rise to the infamous home perm.

Pretty soon cords disappeared altogether, and phones lost their curvy figures. As a matter of fact, they started looking a lot like TV remotes, which amuses the children no end when we use them to try to change channels.

Then the industry went one worse. It made cell phones that can leave home with the kids.

I am pretty sure that children today are born with cell phones included. As soon as they're wheeled into the nursery, they're texting the newborn in the next bassinet over: "nice chook. lol."

Our children cut their teeth on a rotary phone--sometimes literally, once they could crawl within reach of the cord--but they have adapted beautifully to cell phone use. All three are armed and dialing.

We've fielded calls from across the U.S. It's not the locations, but rather, the situations that made picking up mandatory. Guard duty, kitchen duty, duty-free shopping—what better time to phone the folks back home?

We've gotten calls from mountain tops, game reserves and *The Matrix* when it was playing in Marquette. We've been awakened by drunken calls (wrong number, I like to believe) and sobered by tearful ones. It's the gift that keeps on giving.

As irresponsible parental units, we have failed miserably to keep up with either the times or our kids. In our defense, we'd have to drive several miles from home to get cell phone reception. We stay connected with our children on our land line instead.

Unless we can be together with them, in living color.

On a recent and rare occasion, we enjoyed the company of two heirs on a car ride to L'Anse and back. Our joy was transcended only by the anger building in my husband every time another one of their friends sent a text message, causing our children to beep loudly and sometimes in unison.

"Don't those damn things ever stop ringin'?" he finally bellowed.

Our son, seated beside him, bent his head in obvious shame, focusing on the offending cell phone in his hand. A moment later his sister's cell phone rang in the back seat. It was her brother, calling her from the front seat.

You can't buy memories like that. You have to get them with your cell phone package.

18. LAST WORDS

War of the Words

My relationship with Webster's Dictionary goes way back, to a time when I didn't understand something that Dick told Jane.

Our much-afflicted first grade teacher answered my query with, "Bill Gleason, your next stop is the principal's office!" (Bill was always lots of fun), followed by a weary, "Nancy, go check the dictionary."

Webster's Dictionary was located on a shelf at the back of every classroom. It was dog-eared and spineless, with a frayed red fabric cover. The weighty tome held the answers to our universe, as long as we could spell the words correctly.

It was all black and white with Webster, who brooked no deviations from correct spelling and usage. If it wasn't in the book, it wasn't a word.

At first, you checked the dictionary for definitions of words you were too little to comprehend. When you got more worldly, say fifth grade or sixth, you checked the dictionary for bad words, which were of course absent or written in the margins by Bill.

Then you looked for words that could go either way, just to see how ol' Webster handled that.

And he always disappointed, providing serious and concise definitions for words that, whispered in the cafeteria, could cause you to blow your chocolate milk out of your nose.

Who knew that's what they called girl dogs?

Webster had the market on all things defined until 1999, when a new kid came to town. Founded as a parody of Dictionary.com and Vocabulary.com, the online Urban Dictionary was never intended to knock Webster off the back shelf. It just came "natch."

The Urban Dictionary is so far removed from Webster, it can't even be defined without making up a word. It is "a crowdsourced online dictionary of slang words and phrases." Apparently, anything goes in these new Urban Dictionary times, if you can believe its crowdsourced definitions.

For example, take the word, "tight."

Webster defines it as, "so close in structure as to prevent passage or escape." The Urban Dictionary says it's "close, stylish, cool, having everything together," as in, "Me n' Joe be tight since we did hard time together."

I can't help but wonder where I'd be today if my teacher had asked what I learned from my trot to the dictionary and I replied, "Dick n' Jane be tight since they did hard time together!"

While I wonder, let's indulge in just one more trip to the Urban Dictionary, then I'll never go back again, until some youngster hits me up with a slang term that Webster wouldn't waste his ink on. Like "turnt."

Webster doesn't define turnt because it is not a word. Period. The Urban Dictionary defines it as, "The state of being extremely excited, hyped, or intoxicated." To prove its point, the Urban Dictionary provides a prime example: "You turn up to get turnt and there's no in-between."

I think I'll turn in instead, but before I do, you can rest assured that Webster, not the Urban Dictionary, rules my laptop and my writing, because this story has more red in it (spell check underlines) than a Civil War battlefield.

Web' be, like, my frenemy.

Lassie, Come Back!

If you are looking forward to seeing the new movie, *Call of the Wild,* read no further, because I am about to drop a great big dog bomb on Hollywood.

Lassie made me do it.

Lassie was a collie that starred in a long stream of movies and even her own TV show. She was a real, live dog that exhibited better judgement, sense and hair than her long stream of human co-stars. She was even played by several laddies who were carefully trained not to lift their leg on camera.

Lassie was trained by Rudd Weatherwax, who also trained her to fetch his beer and cigarettes, but again, not on camera. She was the darling of the industry with her bright brown eyes, cutely cocked head and her short but pointed barks that signaled, "Timmy's fallen into the well! Again!

And she was not alone in warming the hearts of viewers and raising their expectations of their own pets, who only barked to signal, "I imagined I heard a noise! Again!" There was Old Yeller, Rin Tin Tin, Hi Ho Silver and Morris the Cat, just to name a few because those are the only names I remember.

The important thing to remember is, all of the above were real, live, hard-working animals that earned an honest dollar by acting more intelligent than their human co-stars. Now, thanks to computer generated imagery (CGI), animal actors are collecting unemployment.

CGI animation is cheaper and easier than employing real, live animals. It helps filmmakers meet the high costs and demands of the real, live actors who, and I don't think I am alone in believing this, are more of a handful than the animals.

The problem with CGI animation, as you can tell by the trailers for the upcoming movie, is that it makes Harrison Ford look a little furry. Wait... it's the dog that's computer-generated. And in spite of all its fur, the dog's face is a lot more expressive than Harrison's.

It raises its eyebrows. It frowns with worry. It contemplates tough decisions. It could probably knock out our income taxes, but we already have an appointment with the accountant.

The worst thing about CGI is the method behind the madness. Even though his co-star is computer generated, the actor still needs a focal point to do all his acting. In *Call of the Wild*, it's an acrobat in a blue body suit, bouncing around like a dog.

That would be just fine, too, but we watched the magic unfold with our real, live eyes on a morning news show last weekend. It featured a reporter walking around Harrison's farm, where he enjoys raising acrobats in blue body suits that trot around like horses.

Sorry! Had a CGI moment. No, Harrison has real, live horses, and he is aging mighty well I might add, considering this filly has also left 60 in the dust. But back in the saddle again, Harrison was describing the process of acting with a CGI co-star. It takes a real pro.

Imagine keeping a straight face while scratching the belly of a man in a blue body suit, lying on his back and kicking his leg. As a card-carrying former Maria High School Thespian, I don't think I'd win any Oscars.

And it is not just a CGI dog's world. Movies these days are heavily populated with CGI elephants (Jumanji), bears (The Jungle Book) and more (more). They might behave better on-camera, but they'll never pull the wool over discerning viewer's eyes, and they can't retrieve a beer or cigarettes, either.

I for one will skip *Call of the Wild*, no matter how good the popcorn tastes. In this dog-eat-dog world, someone's got to stick up for acting animals' rights. I'll turn my discerning eye instead to election coverage, because CGI isn't only for animals, and the guy in the blue body suit is currently a hot ticket.

(Did that candidate just shake his leg after his belly brushed against the podium?)

Live Guilt-Free

Your New Year's resolution barely outlasted the ball drop, and now you're racked with guilt.

Join the club! And let's try to get those dues paid before the next ball drops, shall we?

Allow me to explain. I've been paying the dues for a lifetime. It's a denomination thing. And since I have already blown my resolution to be kind and compassionate this New Year, please allow me to make amends.

No, I'm not sending you money! I am sharing my fool-proof strategy for living with guilt. My credentials, you ask? I am a Catholic.

Not to brag (sin of pride), but we Catholics have kind of cornered the market on guilt. We are born sinners. We live and die accordingly. We do a few good works along the way, but there's a whole lot of sinning going on in between.

Catholics can confess our sins to a priest, and receive penance (prayer, more or less of it, depends on the week) to wipe our slates clean. Then we walk out of the confessional, speculate on why the next guy is going in, and bam! We're back in the red again.

In hopes of balancing the budget once more, and maybe absolving myself of that carrot cake I demolished last night (sin of gluttony), here's the goods: The secret to living with guilt is convincing yourself you could be doing a whole lot worse.

Take that carrot cake from last night. Too late, I ate it all! But while I was consuming our garden carrots in their most sinfully rich form, I reassured myself I really am a good person because, "It's not like I ate any lunch."

It's not like carrot cake with cream cheese frosting is a suitable substitute, but I never said my strategy for living with guilt made sense.

It will just get you through your days until the ball drops on this year, setting you up for failure in the following one.

And you can survive that, too, as long as you remember my three magic words guaranteed to deliver you from evil: "it's not like." Or maybe they will plunge you deeper into it. Either way, consider the possibilities:

- Trying to fit $6 worth of clothes in your paper sack on $5 a bag day at the thrift store, when you should be home cleaning your closet? "It's not like I shop Nordstrom's."

- Heading to the cinema lobby for your second bucket of popcorn while they're still streaming the opening credits? "It's not like I get it buttered."

- Hearing the church bells ring on Sunday morning from inside your ice fishing tent out on Keweenaw Bay? "It's not like Jesus didn't fish, too."

I know that last one was a bit thin, just like the ice will be under my feet at the Otter Lake Fishing Tournament this Saturday if I continue to lead readers down this rocky road to redemption.

It's not like they're holding it on a Sunday.

Canada Makes Change

Canada, our immediate neighbor to the north that is known for socialized health care and Celine Dion, has announced a major change. Its change now glows in the dark.

In honor of having been Canada for 150 years, the country recently minted two-dollar coins featuring a pair of canoeists gazing up at the northern lights. In broad daylight, the lights appear green and blue. When the lights go out, they get their glow on.

It's called a "toonie," and according to Canadian advertising, it's the first glow-in-the-dark coin in general circulation. The Royal Canadian Mint has blanketed the country with three million glowing toonies, resulting in a strong bid for a title currently held by Alaska, "Land of the Midnight Sun."

I can't speak for Alaska, and Canada would probably prefer I not mention it in print, either, but some change is good and most of it is bad, and that includes coins people can see right through your corduroys:

"Hey, Bud, got a spare toonie?"

"No."

"Then why are your pants pockets glowing?"

That is the type of hard-hitting question a professional journalist like me would ask, because I can always use a couple of spare bucks, but nobody in Canada asked me first. And it's not like the good ol' U.S.A. has always hit the mark when it comes to minting spare change, either.

I give you quarters.

I meant to give you nickels, but both coins are silver and nearly the same size, and I am forever getting corrected by cashiers who are too young to shop the reading glasses rack at the dollar store.

Back in the good old days, after the Great Depression but before reality TV, change never changed. You had your pennies, nickels, dimes, quarters, and Kennedy half dollars your grandparents gave you for Christmas.

You never spent your Kennedy half dollars because they didn't fit in the gumball machine. That is how Americans learned how to save big money.

Then along came the 50 State Quarters Program, and people started collecting their quarters in commemorative books, just to get them out of circulation.

Each state was invited by Congress to submit a self-definitive design that would appear on the newly minted quarter backs, and more than one dropped the ball. Wyoming went with a cowboy. Minnesota liked a loon. Coin flips--"Heads or Georgia peach?"--haven't been the same since.

Spare change experts predict Canadians will start hoarding the popular toonies, which I think would send a strong message to the criminal element, because your house would glow in the dark. But again, nobody asked me.

The new technology, a luminescent paint, is expected to drum up even more business for the Royal Canadian Mint, which already supplies coins to several countries. In the world of cold, hard cash, the toonie is a hot ticket item.

In the U.S.A., we boast quarters that don't match and dollars in living color, and neither of them make much cents. But we can thank our lucky stars and stripes that when it comes to making change, we can continue to keep our finances in the dark.

Fun With Forecasting

Change is never easy, and it's even harder when it affects our beloved TV viewing. Bring back analog!

As far as impassioned pleas go, that one was pretty weak. I'd have to blame digital transmission.

Government's decision to go digital has pretty much pulled the plug on rural TV viewing. Life as we knew it--mostly news and sports, some HGTV when I could wrestle the remote from my husband's grasp-- just hasn't been the same since.

The decision was made with the best of intentions. Digital TV transmission carries with it the promise of "sharper pictures, better sound quality, and more content." The problem is that the promise, like our picture, isn't coming through.

There's good science behind the switch. It's the application that's causing some static. Digital signals thrive in urban areas, but wilt in the country due to weaker internet, old wires and fewer voters. They get stuck in trees, bounce off low-flying birds, and are too proud to stop and ask for directions.

That's bad science, but you get the picture, unless you live in the country. On our road, we can now draw in just three public TV stations. I can converse at length about lions in the Savanna, but have no idea what local TV6 newscaster Vicky Crystal was wearing during the morning news show.

It's a U.P. thing. Our nearest neighbors, who live 40 acres away and at a little higher elevation, do slightly better. Liz can still see what Vicky is wearing, unless Jim, who lives across the road from her, is operating his tractor. It makes Liz's TV screen go fuzzy.

I and my fellow countrymen can take some comfort in the fact our government is now protecting us from TV in general. But without access to local weather news, there is even greater danger afoot, or afloat.

Ice fishing season in the U.P. typically occurs during the months of February, March, and April if we're lucky. Four inches of ice will support an angler. Five to seven inches will keep a snowmobile or ATV dry. Eight to 10 inches, preferably well-trod, finally pave the way for me.

Fishermen can be on thin ice any time of year, thanks to the unpredictable nature of weather, especially when it's brewing over

Lake Superior. With no weather report to tune into, how is a rural fisherman supposed to know when it's safe to go out on the big lake?

After some careful thought and deliberation, conducted mostly during my morning shower, I have come to the conclusion that we need more shampoo. Also, we need to learn to read the weather by simply tuning in to nature's subtle cues, especially when the weather is foul.

The following is a Fisherman's Guide to Foul Weather. Please be advised that if it doesn't float your boat, I lack legal representation. You can clean me out but you'll have to take the TV too, and then you won't know what Vicky's wearing, either.

Fisherman's Guide to Foul Weather

- **Lightning Advisory:** The lures stuck in your fishing hat keep sparking.

- **Wind Advisory:** The lures stuck in your fishing hat are hanging horizontally.

- **Fog Warning:** The lake looks just like your TV.

- **Heat Advisory:** Your rubber worms are melting.

- **Extreme Cold:** Ice fishing tents up!

- **Unsafe Ice:** Ice fishing tents at half-mast.

- **Tornado Warning:** Your fishing hat is caught up in a swirling vortex overhead.

- **Small Craft Warning:** Small craft are caught up in a swirling vortex overhead.

Good luck fishing! And even better luck tuning in.

I'm Not THAT Shopper

It was in the time of the pandemic, and I was pushing my cart through the grocery store when a fellow shopper happened to glance at the five-pound bag of rice cradled in the child's seat.

She raised an eyebrow--I'd just been rice shamed! --so I beat if for the checkout before anyone else noticed my baby was long grain white.

For the record, I am not a rice hoarder. It's simple math. A two-pound bag costs a lot. Pound for pound, more costs a little less. We've been hitting the rice kind of hard lately because the venison stir fry was a hit, so I made the grab.

If only it was that simple.

Never in the history of mankind have shoppers so closely scrutinized one another's carts, then raced home to register their opinions on social media, sometimes with a photo attached. It's partly due to coronavirus. The rest is human nature.

The medical community was baffled by the initial response to the global pandemic, which was to purchase as much toilet paper as the family car could possibly hold. Its reaction was swift and to the point: it's not that type of illness. But the shelves were already empty.

Next came a run on hand sanitizer, which actually makes sense because it is that type of illness. That was followed by, in order of disappearance, hand soap, paper towels, cleaning wipes, dish soap, trash bags, disinfectant spray, laundry detergent and tissues.

Almost all of the above are still available locally. Nobody wants to be THAT shopper, the one who can't see the checkout through the Charmin, but sometimes you actually need what your fellow man just desires.

Social distancing makes shopping even worse, because it's not human nature for me to throw myself against the spice section, just because there's another shopper approaching and the baking aisle isn't big enough for the two of us.

We avoid eye contact because we feel guilty shopping for brownie mix (me), and pistachio instant pudding (her), when we're both supposed to be sheltering in. Also, we feel kind of silly walking wide circles around someone who is clearly a kindred spirit.

Grocery shopping trips have turned into guilt trips. When we recently needed toilet paper, I grabbed a 12-roll bag and tossed it in my cart. Then I threw a second bag in. Then I put it back on the shelf, admonishing myself with, "Don't be THAT shopper!"

When I get to the checkout, I feel guilty because the cashier has to accept my money without the benefit of a hazmat suit, and let's face it, any one of us could be lethal. I considerately step back after paying, but I have to close the gap again to get my change.

And illness hasn't even entered into the local picture yet.

God and vaccine willing, a few short months from now, sanity might be restored. I'll hold my head high when I need to buy rice again. I'll purchase toilet paper in smaller packages. I'll replace the hand sanitizer in my car cup holder with my 32-ounce coffee cup, fully loaded with dark roast.

And when I ram your cart in the baking aisle because you're lingering between me and the mixes, I'll just smile wide and say, "Excuse me, please. I really need to get to those brownies."

The End!

About the Author

Nancy Besonen is a former Chicago South Sider whose problem with fishing landed her in Michigan's Upper Peninsula, reporting for the *L'Anse Sentinel* to help support her habit. Her weekly humor column titled "Off the Hook" filled vital white space while having raucous good fun with every aspect of Northwoods living, and beyond. Nancy and her husband, Don, have three children and a small herd of grandchildren who provide love, laughter, frequent spills and abundant inspiration.

In Case You Missed Book #1 in the Series...

Back in 1981, publisher Ed Danner took a chance, hiring Nancy Besonen, a rookie reporter from Chicago's South Side, for his weekly newspaper, the *L'Anse Sentinel*. Her humor column, "Off the Hook," was ostensibly all about fishing, but she quickly cut loose, writing about anything relevant to life, especially in the Michigan's Upper Peninsula, as long as it made her readers smile.

There's something for everyone with a strong sense of the ridiculous: "Ask Miss Demeanor," "Life's a Breach" and "Baldness: A Growing Concern." Also, "We Make Hay," "Men Are from Mud" and a particularly sensitive piece, "I'm Poopeye the Sailor Mom." From Michigan's tiniest predator, the no-see-um, to life's biggest challenges, like trying to fly into or out of the U.P., Besonen's on the beat.

"Besonen, a gifted journalist who moved north from Chicago for the fishing and brought with her a deep sensibility for the U.P, both teaches and inspires. This is true nonfiction at its best, both wit and investigative journalism. I am glad she collects it here."

Mack Hassler, former professor of English,
Kent State University for *U.P. Book Review*

"A veteran journalist, Nancy Besonen has a wonderful gift for sweet and tangy, humorous writing and storytelling. She uses visual, nuanced language to paint portraits of Michigan's Upper Peninsula's people, places and events, infusing culture, history and geography. Her colorful tales, filled with wit, action, twists and turns, are a must read for those in Michigan (and beyond), as she inspires us all to think about our own life journeys."

—Martha Bloomfield, award-winning author, oral historian, artist and poet

paperback * hardcover * eBook * audiobook

From Modern History Press

Printed in the USA
CPSIA information can be obtained
at www.ICGtesting.com
JSHW061245170624
64788JS00004B/1

9 781615 998